THERESE RAQUIN

Emile Zola

THERESE RAQUIN

Translated by Pip Broughton

OBERON BOOKS
LONDON

First published in this translation in 1989 by Absolute Press

Reprinted in 2003 by Oberon Books Ltd.
(incorporating Absolute Classics)
521 Caledonian Road, London N7 9RH
Tel: 020 7607 3637 / Fax: 020 7607 3629
e-mail: oberon.books@btinternet.com
www.oberonbooks.com

A catalogue record for this book is available from the British
Library.

ISBN: 0 948230 13 4

Cover design: Andrzej Klimowski

Printed in Great Britain by Antony Rowe Ltd, Chippenham.

Contents

Introduction

Zola came across the original story for *Thérèse Raquin*, one of his earliest novels, in a newspaper article. This was a method of working which he developed all his life: finding true stories, researching the background material in an objective or scientific way, before shifting his point of view to that of the artist.

He even describes the writing process itself as a scientific experiment. First he creates the controlled conditions or environment, then he can observe his characters as they play out their interaction to its ultimate conclusion. In the preface to the novel he writes:

> …my object has been first and foremost a scientific one. When my two characters, Thérèse and Laurent, were created, I set myself certain problems and solved them for the interest of the thing. I tried to explain the mysterious attraction that can spring up between two different temperaments, and I demonstrated the deep-seated disturbances of a sanguine nature brought into contact with a nervous one.

This was a new approach to literary thinking which found allies in the Naturalist Movement, based on theories of scientific determinism which were being developed by his contemporaries Darwin and Taine.

Zola dramatised few of his many novels although he later collaborated with William Busnach on *Germinal* and *L'Assommoir*. *Thérèse Raquin* is the only one to have been produced frequently this century. Unlike the episodic structure of the other dramatisations, in *Thérèse Raquin* Zola tried to establish a scientific framework in which he could observe the passions of human beings. He uses a tight structure of four acts and a single set to enclose the action. The set creates the spatial boundaries which trap the characters in their story. They cannot escape each other, their shared history or their memories.

In this restricted space violent obsession can only change, as in a chemical reaction, into another obsession: sexual desire into a desire to destroy. The ghost of the dead murdered man will never disappear and his presence takes a physical form: Laurent assimilates the dead man's personality and mannerisms. Similarly, Madame Raquin is locked immobile in her own body, unable to accept the death of her son. She can only be released from the paralysis when the truth of the murder is revealed. The story has one solution, one end: death.

In rehearsals we found there was a difference between the four characters who were emotionally trapped in the space and the other three, the visitors, who could come and go freely. In this tension lay the dramatic irony and the comedy which is essential as relief from the harrowing emotional scenes. The play, we discovered, flourishes in the truthful portrayal of huge passions: lust, greed, terror. A huge intensity of playing and courage is required of the actors to make the text live.

My aim in the translation has been to produce a text for actors rather than a literary text. I owe much to the advice and contributions of the cast of the Liverpool production. In performance we slightly altered some sections, but here I have left the text complete.

Pip Broughton, 1989

Characters

LAURENT

CAMILLE

THERESE RAQUIN

MADAME RAQUIN

GRIVET

MICHAUD

SUZANNE

The Set

A large bedroom which also serves as dining room and parlour. The room is in the Pont-Neuf Passage. It is high, dark, in a state of decay, hung with faded grey wallpaper, furnished with threadbare poor furniture, littered with haberdashery cardboard boxes.

At the back: a door; to the right of the door, a wardrobe; to the left, a writing-desk. On the left: upstage, on a slant, a bed in an alcove with a window looking out onto a bare wall; midstage, a little door; downstage, a work-table. On the right: upstage, the top of the spiral staircase leading down to the shop; downstage, a fireplace; on the mantelpiece a columned clock and two bunches of artificial flowers under glass; photographs hang either side of the mirror. In the middle of the room: a round table with waxed table cloth; two armchairs, one blue, the other green; other various chairs.

The set remains the same throughout the four acts.

This translation of *Thérèse Raquin* was first produced at the Liverpool Playhouse in 1983, with the following cast:

THERESE RAQUIN, Johanna Kirby

MADAME RAQUIN, Valerie Lilley

CAMILLE RAQUIN, Sean Baker

LAURENT, Christopher Fulford

GRIVET, Glyn Jones

MICHAUD, Alan Mason

SUZANNE, Anna Lindup

Director, Pip Broughton

Designer, Andy Greenfield

Thérèse Raquin received its London premiere in this translation at the Croydon Warehouse Theatre in 1984, with the following cast:

THERESE, Jane Gurnett

LAURENT, David Moylan

CAMILLE, Stephen Warbeck

MADAME RAQUIN, Eve Pearce

MICHAUD, Seymour Green

GRIVET, Bill Bradley

SUZANNE, Rebecca Harbord

Director, Mark Brickman

Designer, Paul Gambrill

Costumes, Jennifer Nevill

ACT ONE

Eight o'clock one Thursday summer evening, after dinner. The table has not yet been cleared; the window is half open. There is a feeling of peace, of a sense of middle-class calm.

Scene 1

LAURENT, THERESE, MME RAQUIN, CAMILLE.

CAMILLE is sitting in an armchair stage-right, stiffly posing for his portrait, wearing his Sunday best. LAURENT is painting, standing at his easel in front of the window. Next to LAURENT sits THERESE, in a day-dream, her chin in her hand. MME RAQUIN is finishing clearing the table.

CAMILLE: (*After a long pause.*) All right if I talk? Won't disturb you, will it?

LAURENT: Not in the least, so long as you don't move.

CAMILLE: I fall asleep after dinner if I don't talk… You're lucky, you're healthy. You can eat anything… I shouldn't have had that second helping of syllabub, it always makes me ill. My stomach is so delicate… You like syllabub, don't you?

LAURENT: Oh yes. It's delicious – so sweet.

CAMILLE: We know what you like here. Mother spoils you – she makes syllabub specially for you, even though she knows what it does to me… That's true, isn't it, Thérèse, that Mother spoils Laurent?

THERESE: (*Without raising her head.*) Yes.

MME RAQUIN: (*Carrying a pile of plates.*) Don't listen to them, Laurent. It was Camille who told me how much you love it, and Thérèse who wanted to put the extra sugar in it.

11

CAMILLE: Mother, you're such an egoist.

MME RAQUIN: *Me,* an egoist?!

CAMILLE: Yes, you… (*To LAURENT.*) Mother likes you because you're from Vernon, like her. Remember, when we were little, she used to give us money…

LAURENT: And you bought loads of apples.

CAMILLE: And you, you bought little penknives… What a stroke of luck it was bumping into each other here in Paris, I still can't believe it – after all that time! Oh, I was getting so bored, I was dying of boredom! Every evening, when I got home from the office, it was so miserable here… Can you still see properly?

LAURENT: Not really, but I want to get this finished.

CAMILLE: It's nearly eight o'clock. These Summer evenings are so long… I wanted to be painted in sunlight – that would have been more attractive. Instead of this dingy background, you could have done a landscape. But in the mornings I barely even have time to swallow my coffee before I have to set off for the office… I say, this can't be particularly good for the old digestive system, sitting still like this after a meal.

LAURENT: Don't worry, this is the last session.

MME RAQUIN comes back in and finishes clearing the table, then wipes it with a cloth.

CAMILLE: You would have got a better light in the mornings, though. We don't get the sun in here, but it shines onto the wall opposite; that lights the room… I really don't know why Mother got it into her head to rent this place. It's so damp. When it rains, it's like being in a cellar.

LAURENT: Bah! One place is as good as another for work purposes.

CAMILLE: I daresay you're right. They've got the haberdashery shop downstairs. It keeps them busy. I never go down there.

LAURENT: But the flat itself is comfortable though, isn't it?

CAMILLE: Not really! Apart from this room where we eat and sleep, we've only got the one room for Mother. You can't count the kitchen, which is a black hole no bigger than a cupboard. Nothing closes properly, so it's freezing cold. At night-time we get an abominable draught under that little door to the staircase. (*He indicates the little door, stage left.*)

MME RAQUIN: (*Who has finished her clearing up.*) My poor Camille, you're never satisfied. I did it all for the best. You're the one who wanted to come and work in Paris. I'd have been happy to open up another haberdashery shop in Vernon. But when you married your cousin Thérèse, I had to work again, in case you had children.

CAMILLE: Yes, well, I thought we'd be living in a busy street with lots of people passing. I could've sat at the window and watched the cars – that would've been fun… But here all I can see when I open the shutter is that big wall opposite and the glass roof of the passage below. The wall is black, the glass roof is all dirty from dust and cobwebs… I still prefer the windows at Vernon. You could watch the Seine from there, though that wasn't much fun either.

MME RAQUIN: I offered you the chance of going back there.

CAMILLE: Good God, no! Not now that I've found Laurent at the office… After all I'm out all day, I don't care if the street is damp, just so long as you're happy.

MME RAQUIN: Then don't tease me any more about the flat.

Bell from shop.

Thérèse, the shop.

THERESE seems not to have heard and stays still.

All right, I'll go. (*She goes down the spiral staircase.*)

Scene 2

LAURENT, THERESE, CAMILLE.

CAMILLE: I don't like to contradict her, but the street is very unhealthy. I'm afraid of another collapsed lung. I'm not strong like you two… (*Silence.*) I say, can I have a rest? I can't feel my left arm any more.

LAURENT: Just a few more brush strokes and I'm finished.

CAMILLE: No good. I can't hold it any longer. I've got to walk about a bit. (*He gets up, paces, then goes over to THERESE.*) I've never been able to understand how my wife manages to stay perfectly still for hours at a time, without even moving a finger. It gets on my nerves, she's always miles away. Doesn't it bother you, Laurent, to feel her like that next to you? Come on, Thérèse, bustle up. Having fun are you?

THERESE: (*Without moving.*) Yes.

CAMILLE: I hope you're having a good time. Only animals amuse themselves like that… When her father, Captain Degans, left her with Mother, those huge black eyes of hers used to frighten me… And the Captain! – now *he* was a terrifying man. He died in Africa; never set foot in Vernon again… That's right, isn't it, Thérèse? (*No reply.*) She'll talk herself to death! (*He kisses her.*) You're a good girl, though. We haven't quarrelled once since Mother married us… You're not cross with me, are you?

THERESE: No.

LAURENT: (*Slapping CAMILLE on the shoulder.*) Come on, Camille, only ten minutes more.

CAMILLE sits.

Turn your head to the left... That's it, now don't move!

CAMILLE: (*After a silence.*) Any news of your father?

LAURENT: No, the old man's forgotten me. Anyway I never write to him.

CAMILLE: Strange, though – between father and son. I couldn't do it.

LAURENT: Nah! My father always had his own ideas. He wanted me to be a lawyer, so I could handle his endless lawsuits with his neighbours. When he found out that I was blowing his money on visiting painters' workshops instead of law lessons, he stopped my allowance... Who wants to be a lawyer!

CAMILLE: It's a good job. You've got to be brainy and the money's not bad.

LAURENT: I bumped into an old college friend of mine who paints. So I started to study painting, too.

CAMILLE: You should have kept it up. You might have won awards by now.

LAURENT: I couldn't. I was dying of hunger. So I chucked in the painting, and looked for a proper job.

CAMILLE: But you still know how to draw.

LAURENT: I'm not very good... What I liked about painting was that it was fun and not too tiring... God, how I missed that bloody studio when I started working at the office! I had this couch, where I slept in the afternoons. That couch could tell a story or two – what a life!

CAMILLE: You mean, you had affairs with the models?

LAURENT: Of course. There was one superb blonde…

THERESE rises slowly and goes down to the shop.

Oh look! We've chased away your wife.

CAMILLE: You don't imagine she was listening, do you! She's not very clever. But she's a perfect nurse when I'm ill. Mother has taught her how to make the infusions.

LAURENT: I don't think she likes me very much.

CAMILLE: Oh you know, women! Haven't you finished yet?

LAURENT: Yes, you can get up now.

CAMILLE: (*Getting up and coming to look at the portrait.*) Finished? Have you really finished?

LAURENT: Just the frame to go on now.

CAMILLE: It's a huge success, isn't it. (*He leans over the spiral staircase.*) Mother! Thérèse! Come and look, Laurent's finished!

Scene 3

LAURENT, CAMILLE, MME RAQUIN, THERESE.

MME RAQUIN: What? Finished already?

CAMILLE: (*Holding the portrait in front of himself.*) Yes… Come and look.

MME RAQUIN: (*Looking at the portrait.*) Oh! …Look at that! Particularly the mouth, the mouth is very striking… Don't you think so, Thérèse?

THERESE: (*Without approaching.*) Yes.

She goes to the window where she day-dreams, her forehead against the glass.

CAMILLE: And the dress-suit, my wedding suit. I've only ever worn it four times! ...And the collar looks like real material!

MME RAQUIN: And the arm of the chair!

CAMILLE: Amazing! Real wood! ...My armchair, we bought it at Vernon; no-one but me may sit in it. Mother's is blue. (*Indicating other chair.*)

MME RAQUIN: (*To LAURENT who has put away the easel and paints.*) Why have you put a dark patch under the left eye?

LAURENT: That's the shadow.

CAMILLE: (*Putting the portrait on the easel, between the alcove and the window.*) It might have been more attractive without the shadow...but never mind, I think I look very distinguished, as if I were out visiting.

MME RAQUIN: My dear Laurent, how can we thank you? Are you sure you won't let Camille pay for the materials?

LAURENT: He's the one to thank for having sat for me!

CAMILLE: No, no, that won't do. I'll go and buy a bottle of something. Damn it, we'll drink to your work of art!

LAURENT: Oh, well, if you insist, I'll just go and get the frame. Remember it's Thursday. Monsieur Grivet and the Michauds must find the portrait in its place.

He goes out. CAMILLE takes off his jacket, changes tie, puts on an overcoat which his mother gives him and goes to follow LAURENT.

Scene 4

THERESE, MME RAQUIN, CAMILLE.

CAMILLE: (*Hesitating and coming back.*) What shall I buy?

MME RAQUIN: It must be something that Laurent likes. He's such a good, dear child! He's practically one of the family.

CAMILLE: Yes, he's a real brother… What about a bottle of anisette?

MME RAQUIN: Are you sure he'd like that? A light wine would be better, perhaps, with some cakes?

CAMILLE: (*To THERESE.*) You're not saying much. Do you remember if he likes Malaga?

THERESE: (*Leaving the window and moving downstage.*) I'm sure he does. He likes everything. He eats and drinks like a pig.

MME RAQUIN: My child…!

CAMILLE: Do tell her off. She can't stand him. He's already noticed, he told me so. It's not very nice… (*To THERESE.*) I can't allow you to be against my friends. What have you got against him?

THERESE: Nothing… He's always here. Lunch, dinner, he eats here all the time. You always put the best food on his plate. Laurent this, Laurent that. It gets on my nerves, that's all… He's not particularly amusing, either. He's a greedy, lazy pig.

MME RAQUIN: Be charitable, Thérèse. Laurent is not happy. He lives in an attic and eats very badly at that place of his. It gives me pleasure to see him eat a good meal and feel warm and cosy here with us. He makes himself at home, has a smoke, that's nice to see… He's all alone in the world, the poor boy.

THERESE: Do what you like. Pamper him, coddle him, it's all the same to me.

CAMILLE: I know! I'll get a bottle of champagne, that'll be perfect.

MME RAQUIN: Yes, that'll pay him back for the portrait nicely… Don't forget the cakes.

CAMILLE: It's only half-past eight. Our friends won't arrive until nine. They'll get such a surprise! Champagne! (*He goes.*)

MME RAQUIN: (*To THERESE.*) You'll light the lamp, won't you, Thérèse. I'm going down to the shop.

Scene 5

THERESE, later joined by LAURENT.

THERESE, left alone, stays still a moment, looking around, then at last she lets out a sigh. Silently she moves downstage and stretches with lassitude and boredom. Then she hears LAURENT enter by the small side door and she smiles, shaking with joy. During this scene it gets darker and darker as night falls.

LAURENT: Thérèse…

THERESE: Laurent, my darling… I felt you would come back, my love. (*She takes his hands and leads him downstage.*) I haven't seen you for a whole week. Every afternoon I waited for you, hoping you'd be able to escape from the office… If you hadn't come, I'd have done something stupid… *Why* have you stayed away for a whole week? I can't stand it any longer. Shaking hands every evening in front of the others you seem so cold.

LAURENT: I'll explain.

THERESE: You're afraid, aren't you? You big baby! Where could we be safer? (*She raises her voice and moves a few*

19

paces.) Who could guess we loved each other? Who would ever come and look for us in this room?

LAURENT: (*Pulling her back and taking her in his arms*.) Be sensible… No, I'm not afraid to come here.

THERESE: Then you're afraid of me, admit it… You're afraid that I love you too much, that I'll upset your life.

LAURENT: Why do you doubt me? Don't you know I can't sleep because of you. I'm going mad. ME! Who never took women seriously… Thérèse, I'm afraid because you have awoken something in the depths of my being – a man I never knew existed. Sometimes, it's true, I am not calm. It can't be natural to love anyone as I love you; and I'm afraid it will get out of control.

THERESE: (*Her head resting on his shoulder*.) That would be a pleasure without end, a long walk in the sun. (*They kiss*.)

LAURENT: (*Extricating himself rapidly*.) Did you hear someone on the stairs? (*They both listen*.)

THERESE: It's only the damp making the stairs creak. (*They come together again*.) Come here, let's love each other without fear, without regret. If only you knew… Oh, what a childhood I had! I have been brought up in the damp atmosphere of a sick man's room.

LAURENT: My poor Thérèse.

THERESE: Oh yes! I was so miserable. For hours on end I would squat in front of the fire stupidly watching over his infusions. If I moved, my aunt scolded me – mustn't wake Camille up, must we? I used to stammer; my hands shook like an old woman's. I was so clumsy that even Camille made fun of me. And yet I felt strong. I could feel my child's fists clench, I wanted to smash everything… They told me my mother was the daughter of a nomadic African chief. It must be true; so often I dreamt of escaping; roaming the roads and running barefoot in the dust, begging like a gypsy…you see, I preferred starving in the wild to their hospitality.

She has raised her voice: LAURENT, distressed, crosses the room and listens at the staircase.

LAURENT: Keep your voice down, your aunt will come up.

THERESE: Let her come up! It's their fault if I'm a liar. (*She leans on the table, arms crossed.*) I don't know why I ever agreed to marry Camille. It was a pre-arranged marriage. My aunt simply waited until we were of age. I was only twelve years old when she said, 'You will love your cousin, you will look after him.' She wanted him to have a nurse, an infusion-maker. She adored this puny child that she had wrestled from death twenty times, and she trained me to be his servant… And I never protested. They had made me cowardly. I felt pity for the child. When I played with him I could feel my fingers sink into his limbs like putty. On the evening of the wedding, instead of going to my room at the left on the top of the stairs, I went in Camille's, which was on the right. That was all… But you…you, my Laurent…

LAURENT: You love me? (*He takes her in his arms and slowly sits her down in the chair to the right of the table.*)

THERESE: I love you. I loved you the day Camille pushed you into the shop, remember? – when you'd bumped into each other at the office… I really don't know how I loved you. It was more like hate. The very sight of you drove me mad, I couldn't bear it. The moment you were there, my nerves were strained to breaking point, yet I waited achingly for you to come, for the pain. When you were painting just now, I was nailed to the stool, at your feet, no matter how hard I secretly tried to fight it.

LAURENT: (*Kneeling at her feet.*) I adore you.

THERESE: And our only time of pleasure, Thursday
evenings, when Grivet and old Michaud would arrive
regular as clockwork, those Thursday evenings used to
drive me mad – the eternal games of dominoes, eternal
Thursdays, the same imbecilic boredom… But now I feel
proud and revenged. When we sit round the table
exchanging polite remarks I can bask in such wicked
pleasure; I sit there sewing and put on my half-baked
expression while you all play dominoes; and in the midst
of this bourgeois peace I'm reliving our moments of
ecstasy.

LAURENT: (*Thinking he has heard a noise, getting up,
terrrfied.*) I'm sure you're talking too loud. We'll be
caught. I tell you your aunt will come up. (*He listens at
the door to the spiral staircase.*) Where is my hat?

THERESE: (*Quietly getting up.*) Do you really think she will
come up? (*She goes to the staircase and returns with lowered
voice.*) Yes, you're right, you'd better go. You will come
tomorrow, at two o'clock?

LAURENT: No, it's not possible.

THERESE: Why not?

LAURENT: The head-clerk has threatened to sack me if
I'm absent again.

THERESE: You mean we won't see each other any more?
You're leaving me? This is where all this caution has
been leading? Oh, you coward!

LAURENT: No, we can have a peaceful existence, the two
of us. It's only a matter of looking, of waiting for
circumstances to change. How often I've dreamt of
having you all to myself for a whole day; then my desire
would grow and I wanted you for a month of happiness,

then a year, then all my life… All our lives to be together…all our life to love each other. I would leave my job and would start painting again. You would do whatever you wished. We would adore each other for ever, for ever… You'd be happy, wouldn't you?

THERESE: (*Smiling, swooning on his chest.*) Oh yes, very, very happy.

LAURENT: (*Breaking away from her, in a low voice.*) If only you were free…

THERESE: (*Dreamily.*) We would marry, we would no longer be afraid of anything. Oh, Laurent, what a sweet life it would be.

LAURENT: All I can see are your eyes shining in the dim light, those eyes that would drive me mad. We must now say farewell, Thérèse.

THERESE: You're not coming tomorrow?

LAURENT: No. Trust me. If we have to spend some time apart without seeing each other, you must tell yourself that we are working towards our future happiness. (*He kisses her and then exits hastily through the secret door.*)

THERESE: (*Alone. A moment's silence as she dreams.*) If only I were free.

Scene 6

THERESE, MME RAQUIN, CAMILLE.

MME RAQUIN: What, you still haven't lit the lamp! Oh, you daydreamer. Never mind, it's ready. I'll get it. (*She goes out to her bedroom.*)

CAMILLE: (*Arrives with a bottle of champagne and a box of cakes.*) Where is everyone? Why is it so dark in here?

THERESE: My aunt has gone for the lamp.

CAMILLE: Ah. (*Shaking.*) Oh it's you! You gave me a fright... You could at least talk in a more natural tone of voice... You know I hate it when people play jokes in the dark.

THERESE: I'm not playing jokes.

CAMILLE: I caught sight of you just then, all white like a ghost... It's ridiculous, pranks like that... Now if I wake up during the night, I'm going to think that a woman in white is pacing round my bed waiting to strangle me... It's all very well for you to laugh.

THERESE: I'm not laughing.

MME RAQUIN: (*Enters with lamp.*) What's wrong?

The scene brightens.

CAMILLE: It's Thérèse, she's scaring me, she thinks it's funny. I nearly dropped the bottle of champagne... That would have been three francs wasted.

MME RAQUIN: What? You only paid three francs? (*She takes bottle.*)

CAMILLE: Yes, I went as far as the boulevard St Michel, where I'd seen some advertised for three francs in a grocer's. It's just as good as the eight franc bottle. Everyone knows that the shopkeepers are a load of frauds. Here are the cakes.

MME RAQUIN: Give them to me. I'll put everything on the table so as to surprise Grivet and Michaud when they arrive. Could you get me two plates, Thérèse?

They set everything on the table, the champagne between two plates of cakes. Then THERESE goes and sits at her work table and begins to sew.

CAMILLE: Ah, quarter to nine. On the stroke of nine Monsieur Grivet will arrive. He's exactitude itself… You will be nice to him, won't you? I know he's only the deputy chief clerk but he could be useful as regards my promotion. He's a very powerful man, so don't underestimate him. The old boys at the office swear that in twenty years he's never once been a minute late… Laurent is wrong to say he won't make his mark.

MME RAQUIN: Our friend Michaud is just as precise. When he was Police Superintendent at Vernon he arrived home precisely at eight o'clock exactly, do you remember? We always complimented him on it.

CAMILLE: Yes, but since he's retired and moved to Paris with his niece, he's become somewhat more erratic. That little Suzanne is always leading him up the garden path… But all the same I find it most agreeable to have good friends and to entertain them once a week. Anything more regular would cost too much… Oh, I've just remembered, before they arrive, I wanted to tell you, I hatched a plan when I was walking back.

MME RAQUIN: What plan?

CAMILLE: Mother, you know I promised to take Thérèse to Saint-Ouen one Sunday before the weather turns. She hates walking out round town with me, even though it is much more fun than the countryside. She says I wear her out, that I don't walk properly… So, I thought it'd be an idea to go for a walk in Saint-Ouen this coming Sunday, and to take Laurent with us.

MME RAQUIN: Yes, my children, you do that. My legs aren't good enough to come with you, but I think that's an excellent idea… That will make you square with Laurent for the portrait.

CAMILLE: Laurent is so funny in the countryside… Remember, Thérèse, the time we took him to Suresnes?

25

He's so strong, like a horse! He can jump over streams of water and can throw stones to amazing heights. What a joker! On the wooden horse at Suresnes he did this impersonation of a hunt, cracking the whip, kicking the spurs. You know, he did it so well that a wedding party nearby almost wept with laughter. The bride almost had a seizure! Really! …Remember, Thérèse?

THERESE: He'd certainly had enough to drink at dinner to stimulate his wit.

CAMILLE: Oh you! You don't understand people having fun. If I had to rely on you for entertainment I would have a truly tedious time at Saint-Ouen… All she does – she just sits on the ground staring into the water… Now, if I bring Laurent, it's to keep me amused… Where the devil has he gone to get that frame? (*Bell rings in shop.*) Ah, that'll be him. Monsieur Grivet still has seven minutes left.

Scene 7

Same and LAURENT.

LAURENT: (*Holding the frame.*) They always take so long in that shop. (*Looking at MME RAQUIN and CAMILLE who are talking in hushed voices.*) I bet you're plotting some treat.

CAMILLE: Guess.

LAURENT: You're going to invite me to dinner tomorrow night and there'll be chicken and rice.

MME RAQUIN: You greedy pig!

CAMILLE: Better than that… On Sunday I'm taking Thérèse to Saint-Ouen and you're coming with us… Would you like that?

LAURENT: Would I like to! (*He takes the portrait and a small hammer from MME RAQUIN.*)

MME RAQUIN: You will be careful, won't you, Laurent. I leave Camille in your hands. You are strong. I am happier when I know he is with you.

CAMILLE: Mother, you're such a worrier, it's boring. Just think, I can't even go to the end of the road without her imagining some catastrophe has happened... It's awful always being treated like a little boy... What we'll do, we'll take a cab as far as the ramparts, that way we'll only have to pay for the one journey. Then we'll walk back along the tow-path, spend the afternoon on the island, and in the evening we'll have a fish stew by the riverside. Is that settled, then?

LAURENT: (*Fixing the painting into the frame.*) Yes...but we could add the finishing touch to the programme.

CAMILLE: How?

LAURENT: (*Glancing at THERESE.*) With a trip on a rowing boat.

MME RAQUIN: No, no, no boating. I wouldn't feel happy.

THERESE: You don't think Camille would risk going on the water, do you? He's much too scared.

CAMILLE: Me scared?!

LAURENT: That's true, I forgot you were frightened of the water. When we used to go paddling in the Seine at Vernon, you'd just stay on the bank, shivering... All right, we'll give the boat a miss.

CAMILLE: But that's not true! *I'm* not scared! ...We *shall* take a boat. What the devil are you doing, making me out to be an idiot. We'll see which of the three of us is the least brave. It's Thérèse who's frightened.

THERESE: My poor child, you look pale with fear already.

CAMILLE: Tease me if you like… We'll see! We'll see!

MME RAQUIN: Camille, my good Camille, give up this idea; do it for me.

CAMILLE: Please, Mother, don't torment me. You know it only makes me ill.

LAURENT: Very well, your wife will decide.

THERESE: Accidents can happen anywhere.

LAURENT: That's very true…in the street – your foot could slip, a tile could fall on your head.

THERESE: Besides, you know how much I adore the Seine.

LAURENT: (*To CAMILLE.*) All right then, that's settled. You win! We will take a boat.

MME RAQUIN: (*Aside to LAURENT, who's hanging up portrait.*) I can't tell you how worried this outing makes me. Camille is so insistent. You see how carried away he gets.

LAURENT: Don't be afraid. I'll be there… I must just quickly hang up the portrait. (*He hangs portrait over mantelpiece.*)

CAMILLE: It will catch the light there, won't it? (*Shop bell rings and the clock strikes nine.*) Nine o'clock. Here's Monsieur Grivet.

Scene 8

The same plus GRIVET.

GRIVET: I'm first to arrive… Good evening Ladies and Gentlemen.

MME RAQUIN: Good evening, Monsieur Grivet…shall I take your umbrella? (*She takes it.*) Is it raining?

GRIVET: It's threatening to. (*She goes to put it to the left of fireplace.*) Not in that corner, not in that corner; you know my little habits... In the other corner. There, thank you.

MME RAQUIN: Give me your galoshes.

GRIVET: No, no, I'll put them away myself. (*He sits on the chair she offers him.*) I have my own little system. Yes, yes, I like everything to be in its place, you understand. (*He places galoshes next to umbrella.*) That way I don't worry.

CAMILLE: Do you not bring any news, Monsieur Grivet?

GRIVET: (*Getting up and coming centre stage.*) I left the office at half-past four, dined at six at the Little Orléans restaurant, read my paper at seven at the Café Saturnin; and it being Thursday today, instead of going to bed at nine as is my habit, I came here. (*Reflecting.*) Yes, that's all, I think.

LAURENT: You didn't see anything on your way here?

GRIVET: Oh yes, of course, forgive me... There was a crowd of people in the rue Saint-André-des-Arts. I had to cross to the other pavement... That did put me out... You understand, in the mornings I walk to the office along the left-hand pavement, and, in the evenings, I return along the other...

MME RAQUIN: The right-hand pavement.

GRIVET: No, no, no, no. Allow me. (*Miming the action.*) In the mornings, I go like this, and in the evenings, I come back...

LAURENT: Oh, very good. (*Clapping.*)

GRIVET: Always by way of the left-hand pavement, you see. I always keep to the left, like the railways. It's the best way of not getting lost *en route.*

LAURENT: But what was the crowd doing on the pavement?

GRIVET: I don't know. How should I know?

MME RAQUIN: No doubt, some accident.

GRIVET: Why, of course, that's true, it must have been an accident... I hadn't thought of that... My word, you put my mind at rest by saying it was an accident. (*He sits down at the table, on the left.*)

MME RAQUIN: Ah! Here's Monsieur Michaud.

Scene 9

The same plus MICHAUD and SUZANNE.

SUZANNE takes off her shawl and hat and goes to chat quietly to THERESE, who is still sitting at her work desk. MICHAUD shakes hands with everyone.

MICHAUD: I believe I am late.

GRIVET, who has taken out his watch and shows it with an air of triumph.

I know, six minutes past nine. It was this little one's fault. (*Indicating SUZANNE.*) We had to stop at every shop. (*He goes to place his cane next to GRIVET's umbrella.*)

GRIVET: No, forgive me, but that's my umbrella's place... You know full well that I don't like that. I have left you the other corner of the fireplace for your cane.

MICHAUD: Very well, very well, don't let's get angry.

CAMILLE: (*Aside to LAURENT.*) I say, I do believe Monsieur Grivet is annoyed because there's champagne. He's looked at the bottle three times without saying a thing. It's amazing that he's not more surprised than that!

MICHAUD: (*Turning and catching sight of the champagne.*) Well, blow me! You're going to send us home in a proper state. Cakes and champagne!

GRIVET: Gosh, champagne. I've drunk champagne only four times in my whole life.

MICHAUD: Whose saint's day are you celebrating?

MME RAQUIN: We are celebrating the portrait of Camille that Laurent finished this evening. (*She takes the lamp and goes over to the portrait to illuminate it.*) Look! (*They all follow her, except THERESE, who stays at her work table, and LAURENT, who leans on the fireplace.*)

CAMILLE: It's very striking, isn't it? I look as though I'm out visiting.

MICHAUD: Yes, yes.

MME RAQUIN: It's still quite fresh. You can still smell the paint.

GRIVET: That's what it is. I thought I could smell something… That's the advantage of photographs – they don't smell.

CAMILLE: Yes, but when the paint dries…

GRIVET: Oh, certainly, when the paint dries… And it dries quite quickly… But they painted a shop in the rue de la Harpe and that took five days to dry!

MME RAQUIN: Well, Monsieur Michaud, do you think it's good?

MICHAUD: It's very good; very, very good. (*They all return and MME RAQUIN puts the lamp on the table.*)

CAMILLE: If you could serve tea now, Mother. We shall drink the champagne after the game of dominoes.

GRIVET: (*Sitting down again.*) Quarter past nine. We'll hardly have time to get a good game in.

MME RAQUIN: It'll only take five minutes… You stay there, Thérèse, since you are not feeling well.

SUZANNE: (*Cheerfully.*) I am feeling very well. I will help you, Madame Raquin. I like playing the housewife. (*They go out to the kitchen.*)

Scene 10

THERESE, GRIVET, CAMILLE, MICHAUD, LAURENT.

CAMILLE: Nothing new to report, Monsieur Michaud?

MICHAUD: No, nothing… I took my niece to the Luxembourg to do her sewing. Oh, yes, of course, yes, there *is* news! There's the tragedy at the rue St-André-des-Arts.

CAMILLE: What tragedy? Monsieur Grivet saw a big crowd there on his way here.

MICHAUD: The crowd hasn't dispersed since this morning. (*To GRIVET.*) They were all looking up into the air, weren't they?

GRIVET: I couldn't say. I changed pavements… So it *was* an accident? (*He puts on his skull-cap and cuffs, which were in his pocket.*)

MICHAUD: Yes, at the Hotel de Bourgogne they found a woman's body cut into four pieces, in the trunk belonging to a traveller who has since disappeared.

GRIVET: Is it possible?! Cut into four pieces! How can you cut a woman into four pieces?

CAMILLE: It's disgusting!

GRIVET: And I walked right past the place! ...I remember now, everyone was looking up into the air... Did they see anything up there? – Was there anything to see?

MICHAUD: You could see the window of the bedroom where the crowd claim the trunk was found...but they were, in fact, wrong. The window of the bedroom in question looked out onto the courtyard.

LAURENT: Has the murderer been arrested?

MICHAUD: No, one of my ex-colleagues who is conducting the inquiry told me this morning he is working in the dark and the murderer is still at large.

GRIVET chuckles, nodding his head.

The law is going to have some difficulty finding him!

LAURENT: But has the identity of the victim been established?

MICHAUD: No. The body was naked, and the head was not in the trunk.

GRIVET: It must have got mislaid.

CAMILLE: Please, dear sir! Your woman cut into four pieces is making my flesh creep.

GRIVET: Why, no! It's fun to be frightened, when one is absolutely sure that one is in no danger oneself. Monsieur Michaud's stories of his time as Police Superintendent are so amusing... Remember the one about the policeman's body that had been buried in a carrot-patch and his fingers were pulled up with the carrots? He told us that story last Autumn... I found that one very interesting. What the devil, we know there aren't any murderers lurking behind our backs here. This is a house of God... Now in a wood, that's different. If I were crossing a dark wood with Monsieur Michaud, I would ask him to keep quiet.

LAURENT: (*To MICHAUD.*) Do you think many crimes go unpunished?

MICHAUD: Yes, unfortunately. Disappearances, slow deaths, suffocations, sinister crushings, without a trace of blood, without a single cry. The law arrives and can't find any clues. There's more than one murderer freely walking the streets in broad daylight right now, you know.

GRIVET: (*Chuckling louder.*) Don't make me laugh. And no-one arrests them?

MICHAUD: If they are not arrested, my dear Monsieur Grivet, it is because nobody suspects they are murderers.

CAMILLE: So what's wrong with the police?

MICHAUD: Nothing's wrong with the force. But they can't do the impossible. I say again, there are criminals who right now are living, loved and respected… You are wrong to scoff, Monsieur Grivet.

GRIVET: Let me scoff, let me scoff, leave me in peace.

MICHAUD: Maybe one of these men is an acquaintance of yours, and you shake hands with him every day.

GRIVET: Oh no, don't say things like that. That's not true, you know full well that's not true. I could tell you a story or two.

MICHAUD: Tell us your story, then.

GRIVET: Certainly… It's the story of the thieving magpie. (*MICHAUD shrugs his shoulders.*) You may know it. You know everything. Once there was a servant-girl who was imprisoned for having stolen some table silver. Two months later some men were cutting down a poplar tree and they found the silver in a magpie's nest. The thief was the magpie! The girl was released…so you see, the guilty are always punished.

MICHAUD: (*Sneering.*) So, did they put the magpie into prison?

GRIVET: (*Annoyed.*) A magpie in prison! A magpie in prison? Michaud is so stupid!

CAMILLE: Come, that's not what Monsieur Grivet meant. You are confusing things.

GRIVET: The Police are inefficient, that's all… It's immoral.

CAMILLE: Laurent, do you think that people can kill like that without anyone knowing about it?

LAURENT: What *I* think? (*He crosses the room, slowly getting nearer to THERESE.*) I think that Monsieur Michaud is making fun of you. He's trying to frighten you with his stories. How can he know what he claims nobody knows… And if there are people out there who are that clever, good luck to them, that's what I say! (*Close to THERESE.*) Look, your wife is less gullible than you.

THERESE: Of course, what you don't know, doesn't exist.

CAMILLE: All the same, I'd prefer it if we talked about something else. Would you mind, let's talk about something else…

GRIVET: With pleasure, let's talk about something else.

CAMILLE: Why, we haven't brought up the chairs from the shop… Come and give me a hand, would you. (*He goes down.*)

GRIVET: (*Getting up, moaning.*) Is that what he calls talking about something else, going to fetch chairs?

MICHAUD: Are you coming, Monsieur Grivet?

GRIVET: After you… The magpie in prison! Magpie in prison! Has anyone seen such a thing? …For an ex-Police Superintendent, you have just told us a load of poppycock, Monsieur Michaud.

They go down the stairs.

LAURENT: (*Seizing THERESE's hands, lowering voice.*) Do you swear to obey me?

THERESE: (*Same.*) Yes, I belong to you. Do what you want with me.

CAMILI.E: (*From below.*) Laurent, you lazy-bones… You could at least have come and helped with the chairs, instead of leaving it to your elders and betters.

LAURENT: (*Raising voice.*) I stayed to flirt with your wife. (*To THERESE, gently.*) Have hope. We shall live together happily for ever.

CAMILLE: (*From below, laughing.*) Oh, that! I give my consent. Try to please her.

LAURENT: (*To THERESE.*) And remember what you said: what you don't know, doesn't exist. (*They hear steps on the stairs.*) Careful.

They separate hastily. THERESE resumes her bored attitude by her work desk. LAURENT breaks stage right. The others come back up, each with a chair, laughing heartily.

CAMILLE: (*To LAURENT.*) Oh, Laurent, you're such a card. Your jokes will be the death of me. All that palaver just to get out of carrying up a chair.

MME RAQUIN and SUZANNE enter with tea.

GRIVET: Ah! At last, here's the tea.

Scene 11

The same plus MME RAQUIN and SUZANNE.

MME RAQUIN: (*To GRIVET, who's taken out his watch.*) Yes, it took me a quarter of an hour. Now, sit down and we will catch up on lost time.

GRIVET sits downstage left, behind him LAURENT. MME RAQUIN's armchair to the right: MICHAUD sits behind her. Finally, at the back in the centre, CAMILLE in his armchair. THERESE stays at her worktable. SUZANNE joins her when she has finished serving the tea.

CAMILLE: (*Sitting.*) There, I'm in my chair. Pass the box of dominoes, Mother.

GRIVET: (*Beatifically.*) This is such a pleasure. Every Thursday, I wake up and say to myself, 'Why, this evening I shall go to the Raquins and play dominoes.' You won't believe how much…

SUZANNE: (*Interrupting.*) Shall I sweeten yours, Monsieur Grivet?

GRIVET: With pleasure, Miss, how charming you are. Two lumps, remember? (*Resuming.*) Indeed, you won't believe how much…

CAMILLE: (*Interrupting.*) Aren't you coming, Thérèse?

MME RAQUIN: (*Passing him the box of dominoes.*) Leave her. You know she is not feeling well. She doesn't like playing dominoes… If we get a customer, why she can go down to the shop.

CAMILLE: It's upsetting, when everyone else is enjoying themselves, to have someone there who isn't (*To MME RAQUIN.*) Come along, Mother, will you not sit down?

MME RAQUIN: (*Sitting.*) Yes, yes, here I am.

CAMILLE: Is everyone sitting comfortably?

MICHAUD: Certainly, and this evening I am going to thrash you, Monsieur Grivet… Mme Raquin, your tea is a touch stronger than last Thursday… But Monsieur Grivet was saying something.

GRIVET: Me? I was saying something?

MICHAUD: Yes, you had started a sentence.

GRIVET: A sentence? You think so? That surprises me.

MICHAUD: No, I assure you. Isn't that right, Mme Raquin? Monsieur Grivet said, 'Indeed, you won't believe how much…'

GRIVET: 'Indeed, you won't believe how much.' No, I don't remember, nothing of the sort… If you are making fun of me, Monsieur Michaud, you know full well that I find that mediocre.

CAMILLE: Is everyone sitting comfortably? Then I shall begin.

He noisily empties the box. Silence, while the players shuffle the dominoes and deal.

GRIVET: Monsieur Laurent is not playing and is forbidden to give advice. There, everyone take seven. No cheating, do you hear Monsieur Michaud? No cheating. (*Silence.*) Ah, me to start. I've got the double six!

End of Act One.

ACT TWO

Ten pm. The lamp is on. One year has passed without change to the room. Same peace. Same intimacy. MME RAQUIN and THERESE are in mourning.

Scene 1

THERESE, GRIVET, LAURENT, MICHAUD, MME RAQUIN, SUZANNE.

All are seated exactly as at the end of Act One. THERESE at her work table looking dreamy and unwell, her embroidery work on her knee. GRIVET, MICHAUD and MME RAQUIN at the round table. But CAMILLE's chair is empty. A silence during which MME RAQUIN and SUZANNE serve tea, exactly repeating their motions of Act One.

LAURENT: You should relax, Mme Raquin. Give me the box of dominoes.

SUZANNE: Shall I sweeten yours, Monsieur Grivet?

GRIVET: With pleasure, Mademaiselle. You're so charming. Two lumps, remember? You're the only one to sweeten me.

LAURENT: (*Holding the domino box.*) Here are the dominoes. Do sit down, Mme Raquin. (*She sits.*) Is everyone sitting comfortably?

MICHAUD: Certainly, and tonight I am going to thrash you, Monsieur Grivet. Just let me put a little rum in my tea. (*He pours the rum.*)

LAURENT: Is everyone sitting comfortably? …Then I shall begin. (*He noisily empties the box. The players shuffle and share out dominoes.*)

GRIVET: This is such a pleasure… There, everybody take seven. No cheating. Do you hear, Monsieur Michaud, no cheating…? (*Silence.*) No, it's not me to start today.

MME RAQUIN: (*Bursting suddenly into tears.*) I can't. I can't.

LAURENT and MICHAUD get up and SUZANNE comes over to stand behind MME RAQUIN's armchair.

When I see you all sitting round the table like in the old days, I remember, it breaks my heart… My poor Camille used to be here.

MICHAUD: For heaven's sake, Mme Raquin, do try to be sensible.

MME RAQUIN: Forgive me, my old friend. I can't go on… You remember how he loved playing dominoes. He was the one who always emptied the box, exactly as Laurent did just now. And if I didn't sit down straight away, he would scold me. I was always afraid of contradicting him – it always made me ill. Oh, those were such happy evenings. And now his chair is empty, you see!

MICHAUD: Come on, old girl, you mustn't upset yourself. You'll make yourself ill.

SUZANNE: (*Hugging MME RAQUIN.*) Don't cry, please. It hurts us all so much.

MME RAQUIN: You are right. I must be brave. (*She cries.*)

GRIVET: (*Pushing away his dominoes.*) I suppose it'd be better if we didn't play. It's a shame that it affects you in this way. Your tears won't bring him back.

MICHAUD: We are all mortal.

MME RAQUIN: Alas.

GRIVET: Our only intention in coming round here is to offer you some diversion.

MICHAUD: You must forget, my poor friend.

GRIVET: Certainly. Hang it all… Let us not get downcast. We'll play for two sous a game, all right? Yes?

LAURENT: In a minute. Give Mme Raquin time to compose herself… We all weep for our dear Camille.

SUZANNE: Listen to them, dear lady. We all weep for him, we weep for him with you. (*She sits at her feet.*)

MME RAQUIN: Yes, you are all so good… Don't be angry with me for upsetting the game.

MICHAUD: We're not angry with you. It's just that it's a year now since the terrible incident happened and you should learn to think about it more calmly.

MME RAQUIN: I hadn't counted the days. I am crying because the tears come to my eyes. Forgive me. I can still see my dear boy beaten by the murky Seine water, and then I see him as a tiny boy falling asleep between two blankets as I sing to him. What a terrible way to die! How he must have suffered! I knew something terrible would happen. I begged him to abandon the idea of that boat trip. He wanted to be so brave… If only you knew how I tended him in his cradle. Once when he had typhoid I held him for three weeks on end without a wink of sleep.

MICHAUD: (*Getting up.*) You've still got your niece. You mustn't distress her. You mustn't distress the kind friend who saved her, and whose eternal regret it will be that he was unable to rescue Camille as well. Your sorrow is selfish. You're bringing tears to Laurent's eyes.

LAURENT: These memories are so painful.

MICHAUD: Come now, you did all you could. When the boat capsized, by colliding with a stake, I believe – one of those stakes used to support the eel-nets, if I remember correctly…

LAURENT: I believe so. The jolt sent all three of us flying into the water.

MICHAUD: Then, when you had fallen in, you were able to grab hold of Thérèse?

LAURENT: I was rowing, she was sitting next to me. All I had to do was to grab her clothes. When I dived back in, Camille had disappeared… He had been sitting at the front of the boat, dipping his hands in the water…he even made jokes, he said, 'Golly, it isn't half cold. It wouldn't be very nice to take a header in that brew.'

MICHAUD: You mustn't re-awaken these painful memories. You acted like a hero – you dived in again three times.

GRIVET: (*Getting up.*) So I believe… There was a superb article about it in my paper the next day. It said that Monsieur Laurent deserved a medal. I got goose pimples just reading how three people had fallen into the river while their dinner stood waiting for them at the bankside restaurant. And then a week later when they found poor Monsieur Camille, there was another article. (*To MICHAUD.*) Do you remember, it was Monsieur Laurent who came to fetch you to identify the body with him.

MME RAQUIN is seized by another weeping fit.

MICHAUD: (*Angrily, in lowered voice.*) Really, Monsieur Grivet, couldn't you have kept quiet? Mme Raquin was just beginning to calm down. Did you *have* to refer to such details?

GRIVET: (*Piqued, in lowered voice.*) A thousand pardons, it was you who started the story of the accident… Seeing as we can't play, we have to say something.

MICHAUD: (*Raising his voice gradually.*) What! If you haven't quoted that article in your paper a hundred times! It's most disagreeable, understand? Now, Mme Raquin won't stop crying for *another* quarter of an hour.

GRIVET: (*Shouting.*) Well you started it.

MICHAUD: What! No. Damn it! You did.

GRIVET: You'll be calling me a fool in a minute.

MME RAQUIN: My dear friends, please don't argue.

They move upstage, muttering their discontent.

I will be good. I won't cry any more. These conversations are a great comfort. It helps to talk of my loss, it reminds me how much I owe you all... My dear Laurent, give me your hand. Are you angry?

LAURENT: Yes, with myself, for not being able to give *both* of them back to you.

MME RAQUIN: (*Holding his hand.*) You are my child, and I love you. Every night I pray for you. You tried to save my son. Every night I beseech the Heavens to watch over your precious life... You see, my son is up there and he will hear my prayers. You will owe your happiness to him. Each time you find joy, say to yourself that it was I who prayed and Camille who granted it.

LAURENT: Dear Madame Raquin!

MICHAUD: That's good, very good.

MME RAQUIN: (*To SUZANNE.*) And now my little one, back to your place. Look, I'm smiling – for you.

SUZANNE: Thank you. (*She gets up and kisses her.*)

MME RAQUIN: (*Slowly taking up the dominoes game.*) Who's to start?

GRIVET: Oh! Are you sure? …Oh, how kind!

GRIVET, MICHAUD and LAURENT sit in their places.

Who's to start?

MICHAUD: Me. There! (*He starts the game.*)

SUZANNE: (*Who has moved over to THERESE.*) My dear friend, shall I tell you about the blue prince?

THERESE: The blue prince?

SUZANNE: (*Takes a stool and sits next to THERESE.*) There's so much to tell. I'll whisper it to you, I don't want my uncle to know. Imagine, this young man… It's a young man, he's got a blue suit and a very fine chestnut moustache that really suits him.

THERESE: Be careful, your uncle is listening.

SUZANNE half rises and watches the players.

MICHAUD: (*Furiously to GRIVET.*) But you passed on five a minute ago, and now you're playing fives all over the place.

GRIVET: I passed on five? You are mistaken. Apologise!

MICHAUD protests, the game continues.

SUZANNE: (*Sitting again, in lowered voice.*) No need to worry about uncle when he plays dominoes…! This young man used to come to the Luxembourg Gardens every day. You know my uncle usually sits on the terrace, by the third tree from the left, just by the newspaper kiosk? Well, the blue prince would sit by the fourth tree. He would put a book on his knee. Every time he turned the page he would look across at me. (*She stops from time to time to glance furtively at the players.*)

THERESE: Is that all?

SUZANNE: Yes, that's all that happened in the Luxembourg Gardens…oh no, I forget…one day he saved me from a hoop that a little girl threw at me at top speed. He gave the hoop a hard hit and it span off in the other direction – that made me smile. It made me think of lovers who throw themselves at wild horses. The blue prince must have had the same idea: he started smiling too as he bowed to me.

THERESE: Is that the end of the story?

SUZANNE: No! That's just the beginning. The day before yesterday, my uncle had gone out. I was feeling very bored, because our maid is very stupid. So, to keep myself amused, I got out the big telescope – you know, the one that my uncle had in Vernon? Do you know that from our terrace you can see right to the edge of Paris? I was looking in the direction of Saint Sulpice…

MICHAUD: (*Angrily, to GRIVET.*) What! No! A six! Go on, play it!

GRIVET: It's a six, it's a six, I can see very well. Heavens, I'll have to do my sums. (*The game continues.*)

SUZANNE: Wait! …I saw chimneys, oh! so many chimneys, fields of them, oceans of them! When I moved the telescope slightly the chimneys started to march, faster and faster until they fell onto each other, marching at the double. The whole telescope was full of them… Suddenly, who do I see between two chimneys…? Guess! …The blue prince.

THERESE: So he's a chimney sweep, your blue prince?

SUZANNE: No, silly. He was on a terrace like me, and what's even funnier, he was looking through a telescope, like me. I recognised him, of course, with his blue suit and moustache.

THERESE: So where does he live?

SUZANNE: But I don't know. You see I only saw him in the telescope. It was without doubt a long way away in the direction of Saint Sulpice. When I looked with my bare eyes, all I could see was grey, with blue patches of the slate roofs. Then I almost lost the spot. The telescope moved and I had to retrace an enormous journey across the sea of chimneys. Now I've got a landmark, the weathercock of the house next door.

THERESE: Have you seen him again?

SUZANNE: Yes, yesterday, today, every day… Am I doing anything wrong? If only you knew how little and sweet he looks in the telescope. He's hardly any bigger than that; just like a little figure; I'm not frightened of him at all… But I don't know where he is; I don't even know if what you see in the telescope is real. It's all so far away… When he goes like this (*She blows a kiss.*) I draw back and all I can see is the grey again. I can believe that the blue prince didn't do that (*She repeats gesture of blowing a kiss.*) can't I, since he's not there any more, no matter how hard I stare out…

THERESE: (*Smiling.*) You do me good…love your blue prince forever – in your dreams.

SUZANNE: Oh no! Sh, the game's over.

MICHAUD: So, it's us two, the final set, Monsieur Grivet.

GRIVET: Are you ready, Monsieur Michaud? (*They mix up the pieces.*)

MME RAQUIN: (*Pushing her armchair stage right.*) Laurent, as you're on your feet, would you do me the favour of fetching my wool basket. I must have left it on the chest of drawers in my bedroom. Take the lamp.

LAURENT: There's no need. (*He goes out of the upstage door.*)

MICHAUD: You've got a true son, there. He's so obliging.

MME RAQUIN: Yes, he's very good to us. I entrust him with our little errands; and in the evenings, he helps us to shut up shop.

GRIVET: The other day I saw him selling some needles like a real shop girl. Ha! Ha! A shop girl with a beard!

He laughs. LAURENT comes back suddenly, with a wild look in his eyes, as if he were being followed. For a moment he leans against the wardrobe.

MME RAQUIN: Whatever's the matter?

MICHAUD: (*Rising.*) Are you not well?

GRIVET: Did you bump into something?

LAURENT: No, it's nothing, thank you. A fit of dizziness. (*He moves unsurely downstage.*)

MME RAQUIN: And the wool basket?

LAURENT: The basket… I don't know… I haven't got it.

SUZANNE: What! You were frightened. A man frightened!

LAURENT: (*Attempting to laugh.*) Frightened? Frightened of what? …I didn't find the basket.

SUZANNE: Wait, I'll find it. And if I find your ghost, I'll bring him back with me. (*She goes.*)

LAURENT: (*Recovering gradually.*) You see, it's soon gone.

GRIVET: You are living too well. It's bad blood, that's your trouble.

LAURENT: (*Shaking.*) Yes, bad blood.

MICHAUD: (*Re-sitting.*) You need a refreshing infusion.

MME RAQUIN: As a matter of fact I've noticed you've been distracted for quite some time now. I'll prepare you some red vine-leaf. (*To SUZANNE returning with basket.*) Ah, you've found it!

SUZANNE: It was on the chest of drawers. (*To LAURENT.*) Monsieur Laurent, I didn't see your ghost. I must have scared him.

GRIVET: What a lot of spirit that girl has.

Bell from shop.

SUZANNE: Don't disturb yourselves. I'll go. (*She goes down.*)

GRIVET: A treasure, a real treasure. (*To MICHAUD.*) Let's say I've got thirty-two points to your twenty-eight.

MME RAQUIN: (*Having searched in the basket that she's placed on the fireplace.*) No, I can't find the wool I need. I'll have to go down for it (*She goes down.*)

Scene 2

THERESE, LAURENT, GRIVET, MICHAUD.

GRIVET: (*In a lowered voice.*) It's not as jolly here as it used to be. The game was almost jeopardised just now.

MICHAUD: (*Ditto.*) What do you expect? When there's been a death in the house? …But rest assured, I've found a way of bringing back our good old Thursdays. (*They play.*)

THERESE: (*Quietly to LAURENT.*) You're frightened, aren't you?

LAURENT: (*Quietly.*) Yes. Shall I come to you tonight?

THERESE: No, we must wait. Let's wait a bit longer. We must be careful.

LAURENT: We've been careful for a year. It's been a year since I last touched you. It would be so easy. I could come back through the little door. We are free now. Alone together in your room we wouldn't be afraid.

THERESE: No, let's not spoil the future. We need so much happiness, Laurent. Will we ever find enough?

LAURENT: Have confidence. We will find peace and happiness in each other's arms. We will fight the fear together. When shall I come?

THERESE: On our wedding night. It won't be long now… Careful, my aunt.

MME RAQUIN: (*From off.*) Thérèse, will you come down. You're needed in the shop.

THERESE goes out, wearily. They all watch her go.

Scene 3

LAURENT, GRIVET, MICHAUD, MME RAQUIN.

MICHAUD: Did you notice Thérèse just then? She can't hold her head up and is looking extremely pale.

MME RAQUIN: I watch her every day, the rings under her eyes, her hands that suddenly start shaking feverishly.

LAURENT: Yes, and her cheeks have the pink flame of consumption.

MME RAQUIN: Yes, you were the first to point it out to me, my darling Laurent, and now I see things getting worse. Will no pain be spared me!

MICHAUD: Rubbish, you're worrying about nothing. It's only her nerves. She'll recover.

LAURENT: No, she is heart-broken. There seems to be a feeling of farewell in her long silences, in her pale smiles… It will be a long, slow death.

GRIVET My dear man, you are being of small consolation. You ought to be cheering her up, not filling her head with macabre thoughts.

MME RAQUIN: Alas, my friend, Laurent is right. The sickness is in her heart. She has no wish to be consoled. Each time I try to make her see reason, she gets impatient, even angry. She is hiding in her pain like a wounded animal.

LAURENT: We must resign ourselves to it.

MME RAQUIN: That would be the final blow… She's all I have. I was hoping she would be there to close my eyes. If she goes, I'll be all alone here in this shop…left to die in a corner… Oh, see how unhappy I am. What ill wind is shaking our house? (*She weeps.*)

GRIVET: (*Timidly.*) Well, are we playing or not?

MICHAUD: Wait, can't you. Damn you. (*He gets up.*) Look, I'm determined to find a cure. What the devil, at her age she can't be inconsolable… Did she weep a lot after the terrible catastrophe at Saint-Ouen?

MME RAQUIN: No, she was never one for crying. She simply suffered a silent grief. She seemed overwhelmed by a weariness of mind and body; she seemed dazed, like after a long walk, but recently she's become extremely fearful.

LAURENT: (*Shaking.*) Extremely fearful?

MME RAQUIN: Yes… One night I heard her shouting out in her sleep. I ran to her… She didn't recognise me, she was babbling deliriously.

LAURENT: A nightmare… And she was talking? What did she say?

MME RAQUIN: I couldn't make out the words. She was crying out for Camille… Now in the evenings she doesn't dare go up to bed without the lamp. In the mornings she is exhausted, she drags herself around listlessly and looks at me blankly, it upsets me so… I know only too well that she will leave us, that she wishes to join my other poor child.

MICHAUD: Very well, old girl, my enquiry is complete. I shall tell you exactly what I think. But first may we be left alone?

LAURENT: You wish to be left alone with Mme Raquin?

MICHAUD: Yes.

GRIVET: (*Getting up.*) Very well, we're going. You know you owe me two games, Monsieur Michaud. Remind me. I'll be waiting for you.

GRIVET and LAURENT go out.

Scene 4

MICHAUD and MME RAQUIN.

MICHAUD: Now then, my old girl, I'll be blunt…

MME RAQUIN: What is your advice? If only we could save her!

MICHAUD: (*Lowering his voice.*) You must marry her off.

MME RAQUIN: Marry her off! Oh, how cruel! It would be like losing my dear Camille all over again.

MICHAUD: Come, come, let's face the facts. I'm acting as your doctor and as your doctor I prescribe marriage.

MME RAQUIN: No, it's not possible… You've seen her fears. She'd never accept. She hasn't forgotten my son. I begin to doubt your sense of delicacy, Michaud. Thérèse can't possibly re-marry with Camille still in her heart. That would be a profanation.

MICHAUD: Don't start using big words with me! A woman who is afraid to go to her room alone at night is in need of a husband, damn it!

MME RAQUIN: What? And introduce a stranger to our midst! It would cloud the rest of my old age. We might make the wrong choice, disturb the little peace we have left… No, no. Let me die in my mourning clothes. (*She sits.*)

MICHAUD: Obviously we have to find a good soul who would be both a good husband for Thérèse and a good son for you, who would replace Camille perfectly. In a word…well, how about…Laurent!

MME RAQUIN: Laurent!

MICHAUD: Why yes! They'd make such a lovely couple. That is my advice, old friend, they must be married.

MME RAQUIN: Those two, Michaud!

MICHAUD: I was sure you would be amused. I've been toying with the idea for some time now. Think it over and have faith in my professional experience. If, in order to add a final joy to your old age, you decide to marry Thérèse off and save her from this slow, consuming grief, then where would you find a better husband than Laurent?

MME RAQUIN: But they've always been like brother and sister.

MICHAUD: Come now, just think of yourself! I only want to see you all happy. It will be like the good old days again. You will have two children to comfort you in your old age.

MME RAQUIN: Do not tempt me… You're right, I am in such need of consolation. But I fear we might be doing wrong… My poor Camille would punish us for forgetting him so quickly.

MICHAUD: Who's talking about forgetting him? Laurent is forever mentioning his name. He'll still be part of the family, damn it.

MME RAQUIN: I am old. My legs are bad. All I ask is to die happy.

MICHAUD: You see, I've managed to convince you. It's the only way of avoiding a stranger in your midst. You would be simply strengthening your bond of friendship. And I want to see you a grandmother with little ones climbing on your knee… You are smiling, you see, I knew I'd make you smile.

MME RAQUIN: Oh, it's wrong, it's wrong to smile. I feel so confused, my friend. They will never consent. They never think of such things.

MICHAUD: Bah, we will hustle things on. They are far too reasonable not to realise that their marriage is necessary to the happiness of this household. That's the logic we must use to them. I'll speak to Laurent. I'll talk him into it while I help him close up the shop. Meanwhile, you speak to Thérèse. And we'll have them engaged this very evening.

MME RAQUIN: (*Rising.*) I'm all of a tremble. (*THERESE enters.*)

MICHAUD: Look, here she is. I'll leave you. (*He goes.*)

Scene 5

MME RAQUIN and THERESE.

MME RAQUIN: (*To THERESE, who enters, dejected.*) What's wrong with you, my child? You haven't said a word all evening. I beg you, try to be less sad. For the gentlemen's sake. (*THERESE makes a vague gesture.*) I know, I know you can't control sadness… Are you in pain?

THERESE: No, I'm just very tired.

MME RAQUIN: If you are in pain, you must say so. It's not right to suffer without allowing us to look after you. Perhaps you're getting palpitations? Pains in your chest?

THERESE: No… I don't know… It's nothing… It's as if everything in me has gone to sleep.

MME RAQUIN: Dear child… you cause me so much anxiety, with your long silences. You are all I have.

THERESE: Are you asking me to forget?

MME RAQUIN: I didn't say that. I can't say that… But it is my duty to see if there can be any consolation for you. I mustn't impose my mourning on you… Tell me, frankly.

THERESE: I am so tired.

MME RAQUIN: You must tell me. You spend too much time alone and you are bored, is that it? At your age to be constantly weeping!

THERESE: I don't understand what you're trying to say.

MME RAQUIN: Nothing. I was just asking. I want to know what's wrong. I know it can't be much fun living alone with a sad old woman. I do understand. And your room is so big, so dark and perhaps you want…

THERESE: I don't *want* anything.

MME RAQUIN: Listen. Don't be angry. I know it's a wicked idea we've had but... We've thought you should re-marry.

THERESE: Me! Never! Never! Why do you doubt me?

MME RAQUIN: (*Very emotional.*) I said to them, she can't have forgotten him, he's still in her heart... It was they who forced me... And they are right, you see, my child. This house is too sad. Soon everyone will desert us. Oh, you must listen to them.

THERESE: Never!

MME RAQUIN: Yes. Re-marry. I can't remember how they put it...they were so convincing... I did agree with them. I took it upon myself to persuade you... If you like, I'll call Michaud. He'll explain much better than I can.

THERESE: My heart is closed, it won't listen. Please can't you all leave me in peace? Re-marry, good God, to whom!

MME RAQUIN: They have had a good idea. They have found you someone. Michaud is below right now talking to Laurent.

THERESE: Laurent! The person you've chosen is Laurent! But I don't love him, don't want to love him.

MME RAQUIN: They are right, I promise you. Laurent is practically one of the family. You know how kind he is, how helpful he is to us. At first, like you, I felt hurt; it seemed wrong. Then, when I thought more about it, I realised that it would be more faithful to Camille's memory for you to marry his friend, your rescuer.

THERESE: But I still weep, still want to weep!

MME RAQUIN: And I am pleading against these tears of yours and against my own… You see, they only want us to be happy. They said I'd have two children, they said it'd surround me with something sweet and joyful to ease the wait for death… I am selfish, I need to see you smile… Do it for me.

THERESE: My sweet suffering. You know I have always resigned myself, that my only wish was to please you.

MME RAQUIN: Yes, you are a good girl. (*Trying to smile.*) Next Spring will be my last. We will work out a cosy life together, we three. Laurent will love us both… You know, I'm marrying him too, a little… You will lend him to me for my little errands, for my old woman's whims.

THERESE: Dear aunt… I was so sure you would let me weep in peace.

MME RAQUIN: You give your consent, yes?

THERESE: Yes.

MME RAQUIN: (*Very moved.*) Thank you, my daughter. You make me so happy. (*Falls into armchair.*) Oh, my dear son, my poor dead child, I was the first to betray you.

Scene 6

THERESE, MME RAQUIN, MICHAUD, then: SUZANNE, GRIVET and LAURENT.

MICHAUD: (*Quietly to MME RAQUIN.*) I've persuaded him. But my God, it wasn't without the greatest difficulty. He will do it for your sake, you understand; I pleaded your case… He'll be up in a minute, he's just locking up the front… and Thérèse?

MME RAQUIN: She consents.

MICHAUD crosses to THERESE, upstage left, and whispers to her.

SUZANNE: (*Arrives, followed by GRIVET, in mid-conversation.*) No, Monsieur Grivet, no! You are such an egoist, I *won't* dance with you at the wedding. So you never got married so as not to disturb your little habits?

GRIVET: Certainly, Miss.

SUZANNE: Huh, the objectionable man! …Not a single step of the quadrille, do you hear? (*She goes over to join THERESE and MICHAUD.*)

GRIVET: All little girls think it's fun to get married. I've tried it five times. (*To MME RAQUIN.*) You remember the last time, that large unfeeling lady teacher. The banns were published, everything was going perfectly, until she confessed to drinking milky coffee in the mornings. I loathe milky coffee, *I* drink hot chocolate and have done for thirty years now. That would have upset my entire existence, so I broke it off. I did the right thing, didn't I?

MME RAQUIN: (*Smiling.*) Without doubt.

GRIVET: Ah! It's such a pleasure when people get on with each other. That's how Michaud saw straight away that Thérèse and Laurent were made for each other.

MME RAQUIN: (*Gravely.*) You are right, my friend. (*She gets up.*)

GRIVET: That's what the song says. (*He sings.*) Oh dear mother, shall I say, what torments me, night and day. (*Looks at watch.*) Gracious! Five to eleven! (*He sits down and puts on his galoshes, picks up his umbrella.*)

LAURENT: (*Who has come up, goes over to MME RAQUIN.*) I have just been discussing your happiness with Monsieur

Michaud. Your children wish to make you happy…dear Mother

MME RAQUIN: (*Very moved.*) Yes, call me your mother, my good Laurent.

LAURENT: Thérèse. Do you wish to give our mother a sweet and peaceful life?

THERESE: I do. We have a duty to fulfil.

MME RAQUIN: Oh, my children! (*Taking the hands of THERESE and LAURENT and holding them in her own hands.*) Marry her, Laurent: make her happy and my son will thank you. You make me so happy. I pray to the Heavens that we shall not be punished.

End of Act Two.

ACT THREE

Three am. The room is decorated, all white. Big open fire. One lamp burning. White curtains round the bed: bedspread edged with lace, squares of lace on the chairs. Large bouquets of roses everywhere, on the sideboard, mantelpiece, table.

Scene 1

THERESE, MME RAQUIN, SUZANNE, MICHAUD, GRIVET.

THERESE, MME RAQUIN and SUZANNE in wedding outfits enter. MME RAQUIN and SUZANNE have already taken off their hats and shawls. THERESE is in grey silk: she goes to sit: she seems tired. SUZANNE stands at the door and argues a moment with GRIVET and MICHAUD (wearing black), who want to follow the women.

SUZANNE: No, uncle. No, Monsieur Grivet. You can't come into the bride's bedroom. What you're doing is very improper.

GRIVET and MICHAUD enter all the same.

MICHAUD: (*Quietly to SUZANNE.*) Sh, sh, it's a joke. (*To GRIVET.*) Have you got the packet of nettles, Monsieur Grivet?

GRIVET: Certainly, they've been in my pocket since this morning. They caused me a lot of bother both at the church and at the restaurant. (*He approaches the bed slyly.*)

MME RAQUIN: (*With a smile.*) Come on now, gentlemen, you can't be present for the undressing of the bride.

MICHAUD: The undressing of the bride! Oh, my dear lady, what a charming thought! If you need any help with the pins, here we are at your service. (*He joins GRIVET.*)

SUZANNE: (*To MME RAQUIN.*) I've never seen my uncle look so jolly. He was so red, very red during the dessert.

MME RAQUIN: Let them laugh. You're allowed to have fun on a wedding night. At Vernon we used to get up to all sorts of tricks. The wedding couple weren't allowed to get a wink of sleep all night.

GRIVET: (*In front of the bed.*) My word, this bed is so soft. Have a feel, Monsieur Michaud.

MICHAUD: By jove, three mattresses at least. (*Whispers.*) Have you hidden the stinging nettles in the bed?

GRIVET: (*Whispers.*) Right in the middle.

MICHAUD: (*Bursting our laughing.*) Ha! Ha! You are such a joker, honestly!

GRIVET: (*Also giggling.*) Ha, ha! This one will work all right.

MME RAQUIN: (*Smiling.*) Gentlemen, the bride is waiting.

SUZANNE: Look, will you leave? You're getting annoying now.

MICHAUD: Right, very well, we're going.

GRIVET: (*To THERESE.*) Our compliments, Madame, and good night.

THERESE: (*Getting up and sitting down again.*) Thank you, gentlemen.

GRIVET: You're not angry are you, my dear lady?

MME RAQUIN: What, my old friend, on a wedding night?! Goodnight.

MICHAUD and GRIVET leave slowly, spluttering with laughter.

SUZANNE: (*Shutting the door behind them.*) And don't come back. Uncle, wait for me downstairs. Only the groom will be allowed in and then only when we allow it.

Scene 2

THERESE, MME RAQUIN, SUZANNE.

MME RAQUIN: You should get undressed, Thérèse. It's nearly three o'clock.

THERESE: I am exhausted. What with the ceremony, the coach-ride, that interminable meal... Leave that for a moment, please.

SUZANNE: (*To MME RAQUIN.*) Yes, it was so hot in that restaurant. It gave me a headache, but it went away in the cab. You are the one who must be tired, with your bad legs! Remember what the Doctor said.

MME RAQUIN: He said a severe shock might be fatal, but today I just felt so happy. Everything went very smoothly, didn't you think? It was all very proper.

SUZANNE: The Mayor looked perfect, didn't he? When he began to read from his little red book, the groom bowed his head... Monsieur Grivet's signature in the register looked superb.

MME RAQUIN: At the church, the priest was very touching.

SUZANNE: Ooh, and everyone was crying. I was watching Thérèse; she looked so serious... And then this afternoon, there were so many people on the streets. We must have travelled twice round Paris. People gave us funny looks... Half of the wedding party was asleep by the time we got to the restaurant. (*She laughs.*)

MME RAQUIN: Thérèse, you ought to get undressed, my child.

THERESE: Just a bit longer please. Keep talking, just a bit longer.

SUZANNE: Can I be your chamber-maid? Wait. Now, let me do it all. In that way, you won't get more tired.

MME RAQUIN: Give me her hat.

SUZANNE: (*Gives the hat to MME RAQUIN.*) There, you see, you don't even have to move. Oh, but I'm afraid you'll have to stand up if you want me to take off your dress.

THERESE: (*Standing up.*) How you torment me!

MME RAQUIN: It's late, my daughter.

SUZANNE: (*Unhooking the dress.*) A husband, that must be awful. One of my friends who got married cried and cried. Your waist is so small and you aren't holding yourself in. You're right to wear long bodices. Ah, this hook is really sticking. I've got a good mind to go and fetch Monsieur Grivet. (*She laughs.*)

THERESE: Hurry up, I've got the shivers.

SUZANNE: We'll go in front of the fire.

They both cross to the fire.

Oh! You've got a rip in your flounce. Oh, this silk is magnificent, so strong… Why you are so nervous, my darling friend. I can feel you shaking when I touch you, just like Thisbe. She's the cat my uncle gave me. I'm trying so hard not to tickle you.

THERESE: I'm a bit feverish.

SUZANNE: Nearly finished. There! (*She makes THERESE step out of the dress and hands it to MME RAQUIN.*) Finished! And now I will brush your hair for the night, would you like that?

MME RAQUIN: That's it. (*She takes the dress out of the upstage door.*)

SUZANNE: (*Having sat THERESE down in front of the fire.*) Now you're all nice and pink. You looked as pale as death just now.

THERESE: It's the fire.

SUZANNE: (*Standing behind her, brushing her hair.*) Lower your head a touch. You have such superb hair. Tell me, my dear friend, I'd like to ask a few questions. I'm so curious, you know… Your heart is beating so very fast, and that's why you are shaking, is that right?

THERESE: My heart isn't seventeen years old like yours, my dear.

SUZANNE: I hope I'm not annoying you! It's just I've been thinking all day long that if I were in your place I'd be so foolish; so I promised myself to watch how you prepared yourself for the night so that I wouldn't seem too awkward when it was my turn… You seem a bit sad, but you have courage; I'd be afraid of sobbing like an idiot.

THERESE: Is the blue prince such an awful prince, then?

SUZANNE: Don't tease me. You look good with your hair down. You look like a queen in those pictures… No plaits, just a simple bun, yes?

THERESE: Yes, just a simple knot, please. (*MME RAQUIN returns and takes a white nightdress from the wardrobe.*)

SUZANNE: (*Brushing THERESE's hair.*) If you promise not to laugh, I'll tell you what I would be feeling in your place. I would be happy, oh, but happy like I'd never been before. And then, I'd be terribly scared. I'd think I was floating on a cloud, approaching something unknown, sweet and terrifying, with very gentle music, and very delicate perfumes. And I'd step into a white light, pushed forward in spite of myself by a joy that was so thrilling I would think I was dying… That's how you feel, isn't it?

THERESE: Yes… (*Softly.*) Music, perfumes, a great light, all the springtime of youth and love.

SUZANNE: You're still trembling.

THERESE: I can't get warm.

MME RAQUIN: (*Coming to sit by the fireplace.*) I'll warm your nightdress for you. (*She holds it against the fire.*)

SUZANNE: And when the blue prince was waiting, like Monsieur Laurent is doing, I would maliciously make him wait. Then, when he'd come to the door, oh! Then I would come over all silly, I'd make myself very small, very, very small, so that he couldn't find me. I don't know after that. I can't think about it, without feeling funny.

MME RAQUIN: (*Turning the nightdress, smiling.*) You ought not to think about it, little one. Children think of nothing but dolls, flowers and husbands.

SUZANNE: (*To THERESE.*) Is that not what you're feeling?

THERESE: Yes, it is. I'd have preferred not to have been married in winter, or in this room. At Vernon, in May, the acacia are in flower, the nights are warm.

SUZANNE: There! That's your hair done. Now you can put on your nice warm nightdress.

MME RAQUIN: (*Helping THERESE on with her nightdress.*) It's burning my hands.

SUZANNE: I hope you're not cold now.

THERESE: Thank you.

SUZANNE: (*Looking at THERESE.*) Ah, you are lovely. You look like a true bride in the lace.

MME RAQUIN: Now we will leave you alone, my child.

THERESE: Alone, no! Wait I'm sure I've still something to tell you.

MME RAQUIN: No, don't talk; I'm avoiding talking, you note. I don't want to start us crying. If you knew what an effort it's been ever since this morning. My heart is breaking, and yet I must be, I *am* happy… It's all over. You saw how jolly our old friend Michaud was, you must be jolly, too.

THERESE: Yes, you are right. I've got a headache. Goodbye.

MME RAQUIN: Goodbye… Tell me, my daughter, you're not feeling sorrowful, you're not hiding anything from me…? What makes me strong is the thought of having made you happy… You will love your husband; he deserves both of our affection. You will love him like you loved… No, I've got nothing to say to you, I don't want to say anything. We have done the best we can and I wish you much happiness, my daughter, for all the comfort you are giving me.

SUZANNE: Anyone would think you were leaving Thérèse to a pack of wolves in a dark den. The den smells good. There are roses everywhere. Like a cosy nest.

THERESE: These flowers must have been expensive. You are mad.

MME RAQUIN: I know you love the springtime; I wanted to give you a corner of spring in your room for your wedding night. You could live out Suzanne's dream, and believe that you are visiting the garden of paradise. You see, you are smiling. Be happy amidst your roses. Good night my daughter (*She kisses her.*) Good night, little one.

SUZANNE: And me, aren't you going to give me a kiss, dear friend?

THERESE kisses her.

Now you've gone all pale again. The blue prince is here. Oh! It's wonderful, a room like this full of roses.

Scene 3

LAURENT and THERESE.

THERESE, now alone. She slowly moves back to sit by the fire. Silence. LAURENT enters slowly, still in his wedding outfit. He closes the door and advances with embarrassment. Takes off his jacket and waistcoat.

LAURENT: Thérèse, my dear love…

THERESE: (*Pushing him away.*) No, wait, I'm cold.

LAURENT: (*After a silence.*) At last, we are alone, my Thérèse, far from the others, free to love each other… Life ahead is ours, this room is ours, you are mine, dear wife, because I won you, and you gave yourself willingly. (*He goes to kiss her.*)

THERESE: (*Pushing him away.*) No, in a minute, I am freezing.

LAURENT: My poor angel! Give me your feet so I can warm them with my hands. (*He kneels in front of her and tries to take her foot, which she withdraws.*) The time has come, you see. Remember, we've been waiting for a year, been working for a year towards this night of love. We need it, don't we, as payment for all our caution, our suffering, our pain?

THERESE: I remember… Don't stay there. Sit down a minute. Let's talk.

LAURENT: (*Getting up.*) Why are you shaking? I've closed the door, and I am your husband… Before, when I came to you, you never trembled, you laughed, you spoke out loud despite the risk of being found out. Now, you are talking in a whisper as if someone were listening through the walls… Come, we can raise our voices, and laugh, and love each other. It is our wedding night. No one will come.

THERESE: (*Terrified.*) Don't say that. Don't say that…! You are even paler than I am, Laurent, and you are stammering to get your words out. Don't pretend to be brave. Let's wait until we dare before we kiss. You are afraid of looking ridiculous by not taking me and kissing me. You are a child. We are not a normal newly-wedded couple. Sit down. Let's talk.

He sits. She changes her tone of voice to a familiar and casual one.

It was very windy today.

LAURENT: Yes, it was a very cold wind. But it died down a little this afternoon.

THERESE: Yes. The apricot trees will do well not to flower too early.

LAURENT: In March, bouts of frost are very bad for fruit trees. You must remember, at Vernon…

He stops. Both dream an instant.

THERESE: (*Quietly.*) At Vernon, that was our childhood. (*Assuming her familiar and indifferent tone of voice.*) Put a log on the fire, will you? It's beginning to be quite pleasant in here. Is it four o'clock yet?

LAURENT: (*Looking at the clock.*) No, not yet. (*He moves left and sits at the other end of the room.*)

THERESE: It's surprising, how long the night is… Do you dislike cab rides as I do? There is nothing more stupid than riding for hours. It puts me to sleep… And I detest eating in restaurants.

LAURENT: One is always more comfortable at home.

THERESE: That's not so in the country.

LAURENT: One can eat some excellent things in the country. Do you remember, the pleasure gardens by the water… (*He gets up.*)

THERESE: Shut up! (*Suddenly getting up, rough voice.*) Why do you bring back those memories! I can hear them, pounding in your head and in mine, and the whole cruel story unfolds in front of my eyes… No, let's not say anything, let us not think any more. Underneath your words, I hear others; I hear what you are thinking but don't say. Am I right? Just then you were thinking of the accident? Shut up! (*A silence.*)

LAURENT: Thérèse, say something, I implore you. This silence is too heavy to bear. Speak to me.

THERESE: (*Going to sit stage-right, her hands clutching her forehead.*) Close your eyes. Try to disappear.

LAURENT: No. I need to hear your voice. Say something, anything you like, like you did just now, that the weather is bad, that the night is long…

THERESE: All the same I think, I can't not think. You are right, silence is bad, it is better to talk… (*Trying to smile, in a jolly tone.*) The town hall was so cold this morning. My feet were frozen. But I managed to warm them on a little stove in the church. Did you notice the little stove? It was just by the place where we knelt down.

LAURENT: Of course. Grivet stood over it throughout the whole ceremony. That devil Grivet had a triumphant smile on his face. He was so funny, wasn't he? (*They both force themselves to laugh.*)

THERESE: The church was a bit dark, due to the weather. Did you notice the lace of the altar cloth? That lace costs ten francs a metre at least, better than any we've got in the shop. The smell of the incense hung around; it smelt so sweet, it made me feel sick… At first I thought we were alone inside that huge church; that pleased me. (*Her voice getting muffled.*) Then, I heard singing. You must have noticed it in a chapel on the other side of the nave.

LAURENT: (*Hesitating.*) I think I saw some people with candles.

THERESE: (*Suddenly seized by terror.*) It was a funeral. When I looked up I was confronted by the black cloth and the white cross… The coffin passed close to us. I watched it. A poor, short, narrow, shabby coffin. Some poor creature, sordid and destitute.

She has gradually moved towards LAURENT and brushes his shoulder. They both shake. Pause. Then she resumes in a low voice.

Laurent, did you see him at the morgue?

LAURENT: Yes.

THERESE: Did he look as though he had suffered a lot?

LAURENT: Horribly.

THERESE: His eyes were wide open, and he looked straight at you?

LAURENT: Yes. He looked revolting, blue and swollen with the water. And he was smiling; the corner of his mouth was twisted.

THERESE: You say you think he was smiling… Tell me, tell me everything, tell me how he looked. In my long sleepless nights, I've never seen him clearly, and I have a passion, a passion to see him.

LAURENT: (*In a terrible voice, shaking THERESE.*) Shut up! Wake up! We are both half asleep. What are you talking about? If I answered you, I was lying. I saw nothing. Nothing. Nothing. What is this ridiculous game we are playing?

THERESE: Ah! Feel how the words rise to our lips in spite of ourselves. Everything leads us back to him…the apricot trees in flower, the pleasure gardens by the river, the coffin… There can no longer be any indifferent conversation between us. He is at the bottom of all our thoughts.

LAURENT: Kiss me.

THERESE: I understand full well that you were talking about nothing but him, and that I replied about nothing but him. The awful story has formed inside us and we must complete it aloud.

LAURENT: (*Trying to take her in his arms.*) Kiss me Thérèse. Our kisses will cure us. We married so that we could find peace in each other's arms. Kiss me, and let us forget, dear wife.

THERESE: (*Pushing him away.*) No! I beg you, do not torment me. Just one more minute… Reassure me, be good and light-hearted like before. (*A silence. LAURENT walks away, then he suddenly goes out of the main door, as if he's had a sudden idea.*)

Scene 4

THERESE alone.

THERESE: He's left me alone… Don't leave me, Laurent, I am yours. He's gone, and I am alone, now… I think the lamp is going out. If it goes out… If I am left in the dark… I don't want to be alone. I don't want it to be night… Oh, why did I not let him kiss me? I don't know what was wrong with me, my lips were icy cold; I thought his kiss would have killed me… Where can he have gone? (*A knock at the little side door.*) Oh my God, now the other one has come back! He's come back for my wedding night. Can you hear him? He's knocking on the wood of the bed, he's calling me to my pillow… Go away. I'm frightened… (*She stays still, trembling, hands over her eyes. Another knock, she gradually calms herself and smiles.*) No, it's not the other one, it's my dear lover, it's my dear… Thank you for that good thought, Laurent. I recognise your signal.

She goes and opens. LAURENT enters.

Scene 5

LAURENT and THERESE.

They repeat exactly the same gestures as in Act One Scene Five.

THERESE: It's you, my Laurent! (*She flings her arms round his neck.*) I knew you would come, my dear love. I was thinking about you. It is so long since I've been able to hold you like this, all to myself.

LAURENT: Remember how you held me till I fell asleep. And I would dream of a way to stop us having to separate for ever… Tonight, that beautiful dream is fulfilled. Thérèse…you are there leaning against my chest for ever.

THERESE: An endless pleasure, a long walk in the sun.

LAURENT: Kiss me, then, dear wife.

THERESE: (*Suddenly breaking away, with a shout.*) No, then no! What is the good of acting out this comedy of the past? We don't love each other any more. We have murdered our love. Do you think I can't feel how cold you are in my arms? Let us stay calm and not move.

LAURENT: You are mine. I will have you. I will cure you of this nervous fear. What would be cruel, would be not to love each other any more, to find only a nightmare instead of the happiness we dreamt of. Come, put your arms round my neck again.

THERESE: No, we must not tempt suffering.

LAURENT: You must understand how ridiculous it is to spend the night like this, when we have loved each other so fearlessly. No one will come.

THERESE: (*Terrified.*) You've just said that. Don't repeat yourself, I implore you… He might come.

LAURENT: Do you want to drive me mad? (*He goes towards her.*) I have given up too much, for you to refuse me now.

THERESE: (*Breaking away from him.*) Mercy! The sound of our kisses will call him I'm afraid, look, I'm afraid.

LAURENT goes to seize her in his aims, when he catches sight of CAMILLE's portrait, hanging above the sideboard.

LAURENT: (*Terrified, staggering backwards, pointing with his finger.*) There! There! Camille.

THERESE: I told you so. I felt a cold breeze behind my back. Where is he?

LAURENT: There, in the shadow.

THERESE: Behind the bed?

LAURENT: No, on the right. He's quite still, staring. He's watching us, staring… He looks just as I saw him, pale and smudgy, with that twisted smile at the corner of his mouth.

THERESE: (*Looking.*) But, it's his portrait that you can see!

LAURENT: His portrait?

THERESE: Yes, the painting you did, you know?

LAURENT: No, I don't know. You think it's his portrait? I saw his eyes move… Look. They're moving now. His portrait. Then go and take it down.

THERESE: No, I don't dare.

LAURENT: I beg you, do it.

THERESE: No.

LAURENT: Then let us turn it to face the wall, then we won't be afraid any more; perhaps we'll be able to kiss.

THERESE: No, why don't you do it yourself?

LAURENT: His eyes are still looking at me. I tell you his eyes are moving! They are following me, they are crushing me… (*He slowly approaches.*) I will look down, and then I won't see him any more. (*He takes down the portrait in a single furious movement.*)

Scene 6

LAURENT, MME RAQUIN, THERESE.

MME RAQUIN: (*In the doorway.*) What's wrong? I heard someone shouting.

LAURENT: (*Still holding the portrait and looking at it in spite of himself.*) He looks terrible. He looks just like he did when we threw him into the water.

MME RAQUIN: (*Advancing, staggering.*) Oh, just God! They killed my child!

THERESE, desperate, cries out in terror; LAURENT, bewildered, throws the portrait onto the bed, and falls back in front of MME RAQUIN, who stammers.

Murderers, murderers!

She suddenly has an attack of spasms, staggers as far as the bed, tries to balance, but seizing onto one of the white bed curtains, leans against the wall a moment, panting and fearful. LAURENT, hounded by her looks, hides behind THERESE.

LAURENT: It's the attack they warned her of. The paralysis is rising to her throat.

MME RAQUIN: (*Making a final supreme effort.*) My poor child. The wretches, the...

THERESE: It's horrible. She's all twisted, like in a vice. I don't dare help her. (*MME RAQUIN, thrown backwards, overwhelmed, collapses onto a chair.*)

MME RAQUIN: Misery! ...I can't...I can't... (*She freezes stiff in her chair, her eyes fixed on THERESE and LAURENT.*)

THERESE: She's dying.

LAURENT: No, her eyes are living, her eyes are threatening us. Oh, that those lips and limbs were of stone!

End of Act Three.

ACT FOUR

Five pm. Five months later. The room is dark and humid once more. Dirty curtains. Neglected housework; dust, rags and clothes lying around on the furniture, dirty crockery left on the chairs. A rolled-up mattress thrown behind the bed curtain.

Scene 1

THERESE, SUZANNE.

They are sitting at the work-table, sewing.

THERESE: (*Gaily.*) So, at long last you found out where the blue prince lives? Love can't make you as stupid as they say, then.

SUZANNE: I wouldn't know. Myself, I'm pretty smart. In the end, you understand, it wasn't the least bit amusing to see my prince half a league away, always well-behaved like a picture. Between you and me, he was *too* well-behaved, much too much so.

THERESE: (*Laughing.*) So you like your lovers to be wicked, do you?

SUZANNE: Well, a lover you're not afraid of can't be a serious lover, can he? When I caught sight of my prince far away against the sky surrounded by chimney-pots, I thought I was looking at one of those angels in my Mass book who stand with their feet in the clouds. Very nice, but in the end extremely boring, you see! So, when it was my birthday, I told Uncle to give me a map of Paris.

THERESE: A map of Paris?

SUZANNE: Yes... Uncle was rather surprised, too... When I got the map... I set to work. I worked so hard! I drew

75

lines with a ruler, measured distances with a pair of compasses, added, multiplied. And, when I thought I'd found the prince's terrace, I stuck a pin in the map on the spot. Then, the next day, I forced Uncle to take a walk along the road where the house was.

THERESE: (*Cheerfully.*) My dear, it's such an amusing story. (*Looking at the clock and suddenly becoming very withdrawn.*) Five o'clock already. Laurent will be home.

SUZANNE: What's wrong? Just now you were so cheerful.

THERESE: (*Recovering.*) So the map helped you to discover the blue prince's address?

SUZANNE: Mm? No, my map was no help at all. Oh, if you only knew where it led me! One day it lead me to a huge ugly house, where they make shoe polish; another day to a photographer's shop; another time to a seminary, then a prison, I don't know where else… You're not laughing. Come on, it *is* funny… Are you feeling unwell?

THERESE: No, I thought my husband would be home. When you get married, you must frame that lucky map of yours!

SUZANNE: (*Getting up and moving stage right, passing behind THERESE.*) I've just told you it was useless. Haven't you been listening? Anyway, one afternoon, I went to the flower market at Saint Sulpice; I wanted to get some nasturtiums for our terrace. Who do I see in the middle of the market…? The blue prince, loaded down with flowers, pots in his pockets, pots under his arms, pots in his hands. He looked quite embarrassed with all his pots when he caught sight of me… Then he followed me; he didn't know how to get rid of the pots, poor dear! He said they were all for his terrace! Then, he made friends with Uncle, asked for my hand, and now I am marrying him – so there you are! I made a paper bird with the map and all I ever look at through the telescope is the moon... My dear friend, have you been listening?

THERESE: Yes, and your story is beautiful. And you still have your blue sky, and your flowers and your laughter. Oh, my dear, with your blue bird, if only you knew. (*Looks at the clock.*) Five o'clock. It is five o'clock isn't it? I must lay the table.

SUZANNE: I'll help you.

THERESE gets up. SUZANNE helps her to lay the table, three places.

Oh, how heartless of me to be so cheerful here, when *I* know that your happiness has been saddened by the cruel affliction of poor Mme Raquin... How is she today?

THERESE: She still can't move or talk but she doesn't seem to be in pain.

SUZANNE: The doctor did warn it could happen; she was always overdoing it... The paralysis has been merciless. As if she'd been struck by lightning and turned to stone, the poor, dear lady... When she's here with us, all stiff in her chair, her face all taut and white, her pale hands on her lap, she reminds me of one of those awful statues of mourning you see in churches, sitting at the feet of the tombs. I don't know why, but she makes me feel terrified. Can she still not move her hands?

THERESE: Her hands are dead like her legs.

SUZANNE: Oh Lord, it's such a shame! Uncle says she can't even hear or understand any more. He says it would be a Godsend for her mind to go completely.

THERESE: He's wrong. She can hear and understand everything. Her intelligence is still lucid and her eyes are alive.

SUZANNE: Yes, they seem to have got bigger; they are quite enormous now. They look so black and terrible in her dead face. I'm not easily scared as a rule, but during the night when I think of the poor lady I start to shake all over. You know those stories of people being buried alive? I imagine that she has been buried alive and that she is lying there at the bottom of a ditch with a ton of soil weighing on her chest preventing her from shouting out… What can she think about all day long? It's awful to be like that and yet to think all the time, *all* the time… But you are both so good to her!

THERESE: We are only doing our duty.

SUZANNE: And you are the only one who can understand what she's saying with her eyes, aren't you? I can't understand her at all. Monsieur Grivet prides himself on being able to interpret her slightest wish, yet he always replies at cross-purposes. She's so lucky that she's got you by her; she doesn't want for anything. Uncle's forever saying, 'The Raquins, that's a house of God'. Your happiness will come back, you'll see. Has the doctor given her any hope?

THERESE: Very little.

SUZANNE: I was here last time he came and he said the poor lady might possibly recover her voice and the use of her limbs.

THERESE: We mustn't count on it. We daren't count on it.

SUZANNE: Oh, but you must, you must have hope. (*They have finished laying the table and move downstage.*) And where's Monsieur Laurent? We hardly see him nowadays.

THERESE: Since he stopped working at the office and took up painting again, he leaves first thing in the morning and doesn't get home until the evening. He's working very hard – on a large painting that he wants to send to the next Salon.

SUZANNE: Monsieur Laurent has changed into a real gentleman. He no longer laughs too loud, he looks so distinguished. I never used to think I would like him as a husband, whereas now he would be just right... If you promise not to tell anyone, I'll tell you a secret...

THERESE: I'm hardly a gossip, you know.

SUZANNE: That's true, you keep everything to yourself. Then let me tell you that yesterday we were passing your husband's studio in the rue Mazarin, when Uncle suddenly had the idea of paying him a visit. Monsieur Laurent hates being disturbed, as you know, but he made us quite welcome... you'll never guess what he's working on.

THERESE: He's working on a big painting.

SUZANNE: No, the canvas for the big painting is still all white. We found him surrounded by lots of little canvases on which he had done rough sketches, children's heads, women's faces, old men... Uncle was most impressed; he claims that all of a sudden your husband has become a great painter; and he can't just be flattering him, because he always used to be so critical of his work. What I noticed was that all the faces seemed to resemble each other. They looked like...

THERESE: Who did they look like?

SUZANNE: I don't want to upset you... They all looked like poor Monsieur Camille.

THERESE: (*Shaking.*) Oh no... You must have imagined it.

SUZANNE: No, I assure you. All the children, women, old men, they have all got something that reminded me of the person I've just mentioned. My uncle thought they needed more colour, they are so pale. And they've all got a smile in the corner of their mouth.

We hear LAURENT at the door.

Ah! Here's your husband. Don't say anything. I think he wants to give you a surprise with all those faces.

Scene 2

LAURENT, SUZANNE, THERESE.

LAURENT: Good evening, Suzanne. Have you both been working hard?

THERESE: Yes.

LAURENT: I am exhausted. (*He sinks wearily into a chair.*)

SUZANNE: It must be tiring having to stand up to paint, all day long.

LAURENT: I didn't do any work today. I walked as far as Saint-Cloud and then back again. Walking does me so much good… Thérèse, is the supper ready?

THERESE: Yes.

SUZANNE: I must go.

THERESE: Your uncle promised to fetch you; you must wait. You are not disturbing us.

SUZANNE: Well, then, I'll go down to the shop; I want to steal some tapestry needles.

As she is about to go down, the bell rings.

Why, a customer! Well, then, she will be served. (*She goes down.*)

Scene 3

LAURENT, THERESE.

LAURENT: (*Pointing to the mattress left at the foot of the bed.*) Why didn't you hide the mattress? The idiots don't need to know that we sleep in separate beds. (*He gets up.*)

THERESE: You hide it. I do what I like.

LAURENT: (*Roughly.*) Woman, let's not start quarrelling. It's not night-time yet.

THERESE: Huh! So much the better for you if you can amuse yourself out of doors, if you can wear yourself out walking all day long. I'm fine when you are not there. As soon as you come back, all hell opens up... At least let me rest during the daytime since we don't sleep at night.

LAURENT: (*In a more gentle tone.*) Your voice is even more harsh than mine, Thérèse.

THERESE: (*After a silence.*) Are you going to bring in my aunt for supper? No, you'd better wait until the Michauds have gone; I'm always afraid when she is here when they are. For a while now I've seen an unrelenting thought in her eyes. She will find some way of talking, you'll see.

LAURENT: Bah! I get more afraid when he goes to her room. Michaud is bound to want to see his old friend. What on earth could she tell him? She can't even lift a finger. (*He goes out of door to MME RAQUIN's bedroom.*)

Scene 4

THERESE, MICHAUD, SUZANNE, then LAURENT and MME RAQUIN in a chair, rigid and silent, white hair, dressed in black.

MICHAUD: Oh! The table is laid.

THERESE: Why, of course, Monsieur Michaud.

MICHAUD: So you are still living well, I see. These lovers have got a devilish appetite... On with your hat, Suzanne... (*Looking sad.*) And where is our good Mme Raquin?

LAURENT comes in, pushing MME RAQUIN. He sits her at the table to her laid place.

Ah, here she is, the old girl. Her eyes are shining – she is happy to see us. (*To MME RAQUIN.*) We two are old friends, aren't we…? Do you remember when I was Police Superintendent? I believe we first met at the time of the Wolf's Throat murder. You must remember, this woman and this man who had murdered a haulier, and I myself had to go and arrest them in their hovel. Damn it, they were guillotined at Rouen.

Scene 5

THERESE, LAURENT, MICHAUD, SUZANNE, MME RAQUIN, GRIVET.

GRIVET: (*Who has heard MICHAUD's last few words.*) Ah! You're telling the story of the haulier; yes, I know that one. You told me that one, and I found it greatly interesting… Monsieur Michaud has a nose for sniffing out criminals. Good evening to you, one and all.

MICHAUD: And what are you doing here at this time, Monsieur Grivet?

GRIVET: Well, I was passing, and I thought I'd treat myself to a little debauchery; I've come for a chat with dear Mme Raquin. Oh! Were you about to sit down to eat, I hope I'm not disturbing you?

LAURENT: Not in the least.

GRIVET: It's just that we understand each other so well. A single glance and I know exactly what she means.

MICHAUD: Then, you'd better tell me what she means by staring at me all the time.

GRIVET: Wait, I can read her eyes like a book. (*He sits in front of MME RAQUIN.*) Now, let's chat like old friends… Have you got something you want to ask Monsieur Michaud? No? Nothing at all, just as I thought. (*To*

MICHAUD.) You are making yourself out to be so important. She doesn't need you, you understand, it's me she wants to talk to. (*Turning back to MME RAQUIN*.) Now, what did you say? Yes, yes, I understand; you are hungry.

SUZANNE: (*Leaning against the back of the chair*.) Would you prefer if we left, dear Madame?

GRIVET: Gracious me! She *is* hungry… And she is inviting me to stay for a game this evening… A thousand pardons, Mme Raquin, but I can't accept, you know my little habits. But on Thursday, yes, I promise.

MICHAUD: Tut. She didn't say anything at all, Monsieur Grivet. Where do you get that idea from? Let me question her.

LAURENT: (*To THERESE, who has got up*.) Keep an eye on your aunt. You were right, she's got a terrible glint in her eye.

MICHAUD: Let's see, old girl, you know I am at your command. Why are you looking at me in this way? If only you could find a way of telling me what you want.

SUZANNE: You see what Uncle is saying, your every wish is sacred to us.

GRIVET: Hah. I've already explained what she wants – it's obvious.

MICHAUD: (*Insisting*.) You can't make yourself understood, can you, old girl. (*To LAURENT, who has come to the table*.) Laurent, look, how strangely she is continually staring at me.

LAURENT: No, I can't see anything special in her eyes.

SUZANNE: What about you, Thérèse, you can understand her slightest whim.

MICHAUD: Yes, please help us. Ask her for us.

THERESE: You are mistaken. She doesn't want anything, she always looks like that. (*She comes over and leans on the table opposite MME RAQUIN, but cannot stand to look her in the eyes.*) That's right, isn't it? You don't want anything…? No, nothing, I assure you. (*She moves away.*)

MICHAUD: Well, then, perhaps Monsieur Grivet was right.

GRIVET: Please yourselves, damn you. But I know what she says; she is hungry and she invites me to stay for a game.

LAURENT: Why don't you accept, Monsieur Michaud, you are more than welcome.

MICHAUD: Thank you, but I am busy this evening.

THERESE: (*Quietly, to LAURENT.*) For pity's sake, don't keep them here a moment longer.

MICHAUD: Good-bye, my friends. (*He is about to go.*)

GRIVET: Oh yes, goodnight, goodnight. (*He gets up and follows MICHAUD.*)

SUZANNE: (*Goes to kiss MME RAQUIN.*) Ah! Look! Her fingers are moving!

MICHAUD and GRIVET let out a shout of surprise and cross over to MME RAQUIN.

THERESE: (*Quietly to LAURENT.*) Oh God! She has made a superhuman effort. This is the punishment! (*They huddle together.*)

MICHAUD: (*To MME RAQUIN.*) Why, you are like a little girl again. Look at your fingers dancing the gavotte now.

A silence, during which MME RAQUIN continues to move her fingers, with her eyes rooted on THERESE and LAURENT.

GRIVET: Oho! We've become a proper little wanderer, haven't we, with our hands roving all over the place!

THERESE: (*Quietly.*) Great God, she is reviving – the stone statue is coming back to life.

LAURENT: (*Quietly.*) Be strong. Hands can't talk.

SUZANNE: It's as if she's making shapes on the tablecloth.

GRIVET: Yes, what is she doing?

MICHAUD: Can't you see? She is writing. That's a capital T.

THERESE: (*Quietly.*) Hands do talk, Laurent!

GRIVET: By God, it's true, she is writing. (*To MME RAQUIN.*) Take it gently and I will try to follow you. (*After a silence.*) No, start again, I lost you there. (*After another silence.*) It's incredible, I read: T.H.R.E.E.S. Threes! She undoubtedly wants me to stay for a game!

SUZANNE: No, Monsieur Grivet she has written the name of my dear friend, Thérèse.

MICHAUD: Really, Monsieur Grivet, can't you even read? (*Reading.*) 'Thérèse and.' Continue, Mme Raquin.

LAURENT: (*To THERESE.*) Revenging hand, hand once dead coming out of the coffin, each finger becoming a mouth. She shall not finish! (*He goes to take a knife from his pocket.*)

THERESE: (*Holding him back.*) For pity's sake, you will betray us!

MICHAUD: It's perfect, I understand, 'Thérèse and Laurent.' She is writing your names, my friends.

GRIVET: Both your names, upon my honour. It's incredible.

MICHAUD: (*Reading.*) 'Thérèse and Laurent have.' Have what? What do they have, these two dear children?

GRIVET: Oh! She's stopped…keep going, keep going.

MICHAUD: Finish the sentence, just a little effort…

MME RAQUIN looks at THERESE and LAURENT for a long-held stare.

Yes, we all want to know the end of the sentence.

She remains a moment motionless, enjoying the terror of the two murderers, then her hand falls.

Oh! She's let her hand drop, damn it.

SUZANNE: (*Touching the hand.*) It is stuck to her knee again like a hand of stone.

THERESE: I thought I saw our punishment. The hand is silent now. We are saved.

LAURENT: Don't fall. Lean on me. I thought I was choking.

The three gather round MME RAQUIN's chair.

GRIVET: It's too annoying that she didn't finish the sentence.

MICHAUD: Yes, I was following perfectly. What can she have wanted to say?

SUZANNE: That she is grateful for the care that Thérèse and Laurent heap upon her.

MICHAUD: This little one is brighter than we are. 'Thérèse and Laurent have all my blessings.' Of course, damn it, there's the finished sentence. That's right, isn't it, Mme Raquin, you are doing them justice. (*To THERESE and LAURENT.*) You are two courageous souls, you deserve a good reward, in this world or the next.

LAURENT: You would do as we do.

GRIVET: They are already rewarded. Do you know that in this district they are known as the turtle doves?

MICHAUD: Ah, and it was *we* who married them... Are you coming Monsieur Grivet? We must let them get on with their supper, after all. (*Coming back to MME RAQUIN.*) Have patience, old girl. Your little hands will come back to life, and your legs too. It's a good sign to have been able to move your fingers just a little; your recovery is near at hand. Goodbye. (*He leaves.*)

SUZANNE: (*To THERESE.*) Till tomorrow, good friend. (*She leaves.*)

GRIVET: (*To MME RAQUIN.*) There, I said we understood each other perfectly. Take courage, we will start up our Thursday dominoes again, and we will beat Monsieur Michaud between the two of us; yes, we will thrash him. (*On his way out, to THERESE and LAURENT.*) Goodbye, turtle doves, you are two turtle doves.

As MICHAUD, SUZANNE and GRIVET leave by the spiral staircase, THERESE goes out of the upstage door and returns with the soup.

Scene 6

THERESE, LAURENT, MME RAQUIN.

During this scene, MME RAQUIN's face reflects the emotions that she is feeling: anger, horror, and joy, total revenge. Her burning eyes hound the murderers, sharing their outbursts and sobs.

LAURENT: She would have given us up.

THERESE: Shut up, leave her alone. (*She serves the soup.*)

LAURENT: (*Sitting at the table upstage.*) Do you think she would spare us if she could speak: Michaud and Grivet had a peculiar smile on their faces when they were talking about our happiness. They'll end up knowing everything, you'll see. Grivet put his hat on to one side, didn't he?

THERESE: (*Putting down the soup tureen.*) Yes, I believe so.

LAURENT: He buttoned his frock-coat and he put a hand into his pocket on his way out. At the office he always used to button his frock-coat like that when he wanted to look important. And the way he said, 'Goodbye, turtle doves'. The imbecile.

THERESE: (*Coming back.*) Be quiet; don't make it worse than it already is.

LAURENT: When he twists his mouth in that stupid manner, you know, it must be to laugh at us. I don't trust these people who play the fool… They know everything, I assure you.

THERESE: They are too innocent… It would be one end, if they gave us up; but they see nothing, they will continue to traipse through our pitiful lives with their oblivious bourgeois tread. (*She sits at the table.*) Let us talk about something else. You must be mad to raise the subject when she is still here.

LAURENT: I haven't got a spoon.

THERESE goes and fetches a spoon from the sideboard, gives it to LAURENT and sits.

Are you not going to feed her?

THERESE: Yes, when I've finished my soup.

LAURENT: (*Tasting the soup.*) Your soup is dreadful, it's too salty. (*He pushes it away.*) It's one of your wicked tricks. You know I hate salt.

THERESE: Laurent, please don't pick an argument with me. I am very tired. The tension just now has left me shattered.

LAURENT: Yes, make yourself listless…you torture me with your petty annoyances.

THERESE: You want us to have a quarrel, don't you?

LAURENT: I 'want' you to stop talking to me in that tone of voice.

THERESE: Oh really! (*In a rough voice, pushing away her plate.*) Very well, just as you please, we will not eat any more this evening, we will tear each other apart, and my aunt can listen. It's a treat we give her every day now.

LAURENT: Do you calculate the blows you give me? Why, you spy on me, you try to touch my open wounds and then you are happy when the pain drives me mad.

THERESE: It wasn't me who found the soup too salty! Here we go! The most ridiculous pretext is enough, isn't it! You just want to argue all evening, to dull your nerves so that you can sleep a little during the night.

LAURENT: You don't sleep any more than I do.

THERESE: Oh, you have made my whole existence appalling. As soon as night falls, we begin to shake. You know who is there, between us. Oh, what torture it is in this room!

LAURENT: It's your fault.

THERESE: My fault! Is it my fault if, instead of the rich life you dreamt of, all you have created is fear and disgust?

LAURENT: Yes, it's your fault.

THERESE: Stop it! I am not an idiot! Don't think I don't know you. You've always been a calculating thing. When you took me as your mistress, it was because I didn't cost anything… You don't even dare deny it… Oh, don't you see, I hate you!

LAURENT: Who's looking for a quarrel now, me or you?

THERESE: I hate you. You killed Camille!

LAURENT: (*Gets up and sits down again.*) Be quiet! (*Pointing to MME RAQUIN.*) A moment ago, you told me to be silent in front of her. Do not force me to recall the facts, to tell the truth all over again in her presence.

THERESE: Oh, let her hear, let her suffer! Haven't I suffered? The *truth* is that you killed Camille.

LAURENT: You're lying, admit that you are lying… If I threw him into the river, it was because you pushed me into the murder.

THERESE: Me? Me?

LAURENT: Yes, you. Don't play the innocent, don't make me drag it from you by force… I need you to confess to your crime, I need you to accept your share of the guilt. That gives me relief and calms me.

THERESE: But it wasn't I who killed Camille.

LAURENT: Yes it was, a thousand times yes! You were on the bank, and I said to you quietly, 'I am going to throw him into the river.' You consented, you got into the boat… You see very well that you killed him with me.

THERESE: That's not true… I was mad, I don't know what I did any more. I never wanted to kill him.

LAURENT: And, in the middle of the Seine, when I capsized the boat, didn't I warn you? You grabbed onto my neck. You left him to drown *like a dog.*

THERESE: It is not true, you killed him!

LAURENT: And, in the cab on the way back, didn't you put your hand into mine? Your hand fired my heart.

THERESE: *You* killed him.

LAURENT: (*To MME RAQUIN.*) She doesn't remember. She's deliberately not remembering. (*To THERESE.*) You intoxicated me with your caresses, here, in this room. You pushed me against your husband, you wanted to get rid of him. He didn't please you, he used to shiver with fever, you said. Three years ago was I like this? Was I a wretch then? I used to be an upright gentleman, I didn't do any harm to anyone… I wouldn't have even crushed a fly.

THERESE: *You* killed him!

LAURENT: Twice you turned me into a cruel brute… I used to be prudent and peaceful. And look at me now, I tremble at the least shadow like an easily-frightened child. My nerves are just as wretched as yours. You have led me to adultery, to murder, without my even noticing. Now when I look back, I remain stupefied by what I have done. In my dreams I see policemen, the court, the guillotine, pass before my eyes. (*He rises.*) You play the innocent in vain – at night your teeth chatter with terror. You know very well that if the ghost were to come, he would strangle you first.

THERESE: (*Getting up.*) Don't say that. You killed him. (*Both standing at the table.*)

LAURENT: Listen, it is cowardly to refuse your share of the crime. You want to make my guilt the heavier, don't you? Since you push me to the edge, I prefer to make an end of it. You see, I am quite calm. (*He takes his hat.*) I am going to tell the whole story to the Police Superintendent for the area.

THERESE: (*Jeering.*) What a good idea!

LAURENT: We will *both* be arrested, we will soon see what the judge thinks of your innocence.

THERESE: Do you think you can scare me? I am more weary than you. I am the one who will go to the magistrate, if you don't.

LAURENT: I don't need you to accompany me – I will be able to tell them everything myself.

THERESE: Oh no, every time we quarrel, when you run out of reasons, you always bring up this threat. Well, today I want it to be serious. I am not a coward, like you. I am ready to follow you to the scaffold. Come on, let's go, I'll come with you. (*She goes with him as far as the spiral staircase.*)

LAURENT: (*Stammering.*) As you wish, we'll go together to the police.

He goes down – THERESE remains immobile, listening; she is gradually seized by a fit of shaking and terror – MME RAQUIN turns her head, her face lit up by a fierce smile.

THERESE: He's gone down. He's still down there. Will he have the courage to give us up? …I don't want that, I will run after him, grab his arm and bring him back… And what if he shouts out the whole story in the street. Oh, my God, I was wrong to push him to the limit. I should have been more reasonable… (*Listening.*) He's stopped in the shop, the bell hasn't rung. What can he be doing? He's coming back up, oh I can hear him coming back up the stairs. I knew he was too much of a coward. (*Suddenly.*) The coward! Coward!

LAURENT: (*Coming in, sits down. He is broken, head in his hands.*) I can't, I can't.

THERESE: (*In a mocking tone.*) Oh! Back already, are you? What did they say? Oh, how I pity you, you have no blood in your veins.

LAURENT: (*In a lower voice.*) I can't.

THERESE: You ought to be helping me to carry the terrible memory, but you are feebler than I am… How can you ask us to forget?

LAURENT: So you accept your part of the crime now, do you?

THERESE: Yes. I am guilty. If you like, I am more guilty than you. I should have saved my husband from your clutches. Camille was so good.

LAURENT: Let's not start again, I beg you. How you revel when you have driven me frantic. Don't look at me. Stop smiling. I will escape from you when I wish to. (*He takes out a little bottle from his pocket.*) Here is the remission, here is the peaceful sleep. Two drops of prussic acid will be enough.

THERESE: Poison! Oh no, you are too cowardly. I dare you to drink it. Drink, go on, Laurent, drink just a little, to see…

LAURENT: Be quiet. Don't push me any further.

THERESE: I am calm, you won't drink it… Camille was good, do you hear, and I wish you were in his place in the ground

LAURENT: Be quiet!

THERESE: Why, you don't know a woman's heart. How can you expect me not to hate you, drenched as you are in Camille's blood?

LAURENT: (*Pacing back and forth, as if hallucinating.*) Will you be quiet! I can hear something hammering in my head. It will shatter my skull… What is this infernal game of yours, to have regrets now, to weep louder and louder? I am living with him all the time now. He did this, he did that, he was good, he was generous. Oh, misery! I am going mad… He is living with us. He sits on my chair, he sits at the table next to me, uses our furniture. He used to eat off my plate, he's still eating off it. I don't know any more, I am him, I am Camille… I've got his wife, I've got his place at table, I've got his sheets. I am Camille, Camille, Camille!

THERESE: It's a cruel game *you're* playing putting his face in all your paintings.

LAURENT: Oh, so you know that, do you? (*Lowering his voice.*) Talk softer, it's terrible, my hands are no longer my own. I can't even paint any more, it's always his face that takes shape under my hand. No, these hands are no longer mine. They will kill me in the end, if I don't cut them off. They are his hands, he has taken them from me.

THERESE: It's the punishment.

LAURENT: Tell me I haven't got Camille's mouth. (*He kisses her.*) Look, did you hear that? I pronounced that phrase just as Camille would have done. Listen, 'I've got his mouth. I've got his mouth.' That's it, isn't it? I talk like him, I laugh like him. He is always there, in my head, punching with his clenched fists.

THERESE: It is the punishment.

LAURENT: (*Violently.*) Go away woman, you are driving me mad. Go away, or I'll… (*He throws her to the ground in front of the table and raises his foot.*)

THERESE: (*On the ground.*) Kill me, like the other, make an end of it all… Camille never laid a hand on me. You, you are a monster… But kill me, like the other!

LAURENT, demented, backs away and breaks upstage. He sits down, his head in his hands. Meanwhile, MME RAQUIN manages to push a knife off the table, which lands in front of THERESE. THERESE slowly turns her head at this noise: she looks in turn at MME RAQUIN and at the knife.

You pushed it and made it fall. Your eyes are burning like two hell-holes. I know what you are saying. You are right, this man is making my existence intolerable. If he wasn't always there, reminding me of what I long to forget, I would be peaceful, I would work out a gentle life for myself. (*To MME RAQUIN, as she picks up the knife.*) You're looking at the knife, aren't you? Yes. I am holding the knife and I don't want this man to torture me any longer… He killed Camille, who was in his way… He is in my way! (*She gets up, with the knife in her fist.*)

LAURENT: (*Who gets up, hiding the bottle of poison in his hand.*) Let us make peace, let us finish our meal, shall we?

THERESE: If you like. (*To herself.*) I will never be patient enough to wait till night. The knife is burning my hand.

LAURENT: What are you thinking about? Sit down at the table… Wait, I will serve you with something to drink. (*He pours some water into a glass.*)

THERESE: Better to end it all now. (*She approaches with the knife raised. But she sees LAURENT pour the poison into the glass.*) What are you pouring into it, Laurent?

LAURENT: (*Likewise sees the knife.*) Why are you raising your arm?

A silence.

Drop the knife!

THERESE: Drop the poison.

They look at each other with a terrible stare: then they let the bottle and knife drop.

LAURENT: At the same moment, in each mind, the same thought, the horrible thought.

THERESE: Remember how we adored each other with such passionate kisses, Laurent? And here we are, face to face, with poison and a knife. (*She glances towards MME RAQUIN and shrieks with shock.*) Laurent, look!

LAURENT: (*Getting up and turning towards MME RAQUIN with terror.*) She was there, waiting to watch us die!

THERESE: But can't you see her lips are moving? She is smiling… Oh, what a terrible smile!

LAURENT: She's coming back to life.

THERESE: She's going to speak, I tell you, she's going to speak!

LAURENT: I know how to stop her. (*He goes to leap on MME RAQUIN when she slowly rises to her feet. He staggers back, reeling.*)

MME RAQUIN: (*Standing up, in a low, deep voice.*) Murderer of the child, dare to strike the mother!

THERESE: Oh mercy! Don't hand us over to the police.

MME RAQUIN: Hand you over! No, no… I thought of it, just now when I regained my strength. I began to write your act of indictment on the table. But I stopped myself; I thought that human justice would be too quick. And I want to watch your slow death, here in this room, where you stole from me all my happiness.

THERESE: (*Sobbing, throwing herself at MME RAQUIN's feet.*) Forgive me… My fears are suffocating me… I am a miserable wretch… If you wish to raise your foot, I will deliver up my head, on the floor – here, so that you can crush it… Pity…have pity!

MME RAQUIN: (*Leaning on the table.*) Pity? Did you have any for the poor child I adored? Don't ask for pity. I have no more pity. You have torn out my heart.

LAURENT falls to his knees.

I will not save you from each other. May your remorse make you lash out at each other like enraged beasts. I shall not give you up to justice. You are mine, only mine, and I am watching over you.

THERESE: It is too much not to be punished… We will judge each other, and we will condemn each other.

She picks up the bottle of prussic acid, drinks greedily and falls to the ground at MME RAQUIN's feet. LAURENT, who has seized the bottle, also drinks and falls.

MME RAQUIN stands over them, watching.

MME RAQUIN: Dead. They're dead.

The End.